Beginning . . .

I just love dancing to the rhythm of the Universe!!!!
Every day is such a blessing . . .

Laughter is the music of the Universe . . .

What else is possible? Stay in the question and
watch your life open before your eyes!!!

Life is filled with wonder, miracles, love, passion.
It is limitless, ever changing and expanding every
day in every way.

Living in gratitude is the key to a happy life. If you
are grateful, you simply cannot be angry,
depressed or frustrated!!! It's impossible!

Though it may not always seem like it, our
challenges in life serve a purpose in the evolution
of ourselves, our souls. Without challenges, we
would be empty, never striving toward another
level of inner growth, remaining stagnant, and
unable to achieve our maximum potential.

Life would be so much happier if we looked upon
each day as brand new, never having experienced
anything before--understanding that we really
know nothing--and being thankful for each
moment that we experience, knowing that every
person, every moment, every situation, plays a
part in the theatre of life, and the Universe is our
grand audience, always giving us a standing
ovation.

We are all a tiny cog in the wheel of The Universe. All of our problems, everything that troubles us, are really quite meaningless in the long scheme of things. We are not even a grain of sand in the Universe. Not even a blink in the eye of the Universe. Yet, we are all needed to make The Universe complete. Crazy, huh?

The human body is a magnificent machine. It is perfect in its design. When it needs fuel, we feed it. When it needs repair, we fix it. When it needs rest, we sleep. And, almost always, the body bounces back to an amazing state of perfection.

We're born. We die. The journey is what is in between. Live the journey, not the ultimate destination!

People weave in and out of our lives from the time we're born. Everyone who has touched our life has served some sort of a purpose. Kind of like each grain of sand on a beach serves a purpose. If you keep taking away grains of sand, there will be no beach. If we keep people out of our lives, we will be empty shells. Everyone has something to bring to the table in our life.

The trick is not to take anyone or anything for granted. It's not necessarily so easy . . . We all tend to take our spouses for granted, our siblings, our children, our homes, the food we eat, our jobs, even our pets. I vote for an "I appreciate everything" day -- perhaps it should be every day. Maybe we all just need to be a little more aware of everything. . . what do you think?

When we see qualities in another it is often because we either have or desire those same qualities. If we see qualities in another that we dislike, we can be looking in a mirror – as we often possess those very same qualities that we dislike in another. By the same token, when we like someone, often we possess those qualities or we would like to possess those same qualities. Either way, we must always look within to change, whether it be something we wish to undo or something we strive to be.

Our karmic journeys are amazing: The things that are easy for us to do are our karmic rewards. All of the things that we find challenging are the things that we have to work on in this lifetime. Life would be boring if we were able to do everything we wanted to do without even a little challenge. How nice of the universe to keep this in mind . . . allowing us to continually grow spiritually while on our karmic journeys.

People think they don't pray. Thought = Prayer. We all think, therefore we all pray, whether or not we want to call it prayer -- well, that's something else . . .

How fascinating it is when we meet people and we just know, I mean really deep down inside know, that we will be friends with them forever. I'm grateful that my journey in life has brought me many places to meet wonderful people who are my "forever" friends. And they can live half-way around the world-it doesn't matter, you are still friends. Friendship. What a wonderful karmic gift from the Universe.

We often want to see the good in others and want them to be other than what they have demonstrated themselves to be. All I can say is when someone shows you their true colors, believe them.

Whenever I'm on line at the store or walking down the streets in town, I strike up conversations with people or say hello to those whom I pass. While speaking with someone, I make it a point to keep the conversation positive and always try to pay a compliment. We are never fully aware of how we can affect someone's life by paying them a small compliment or by saying good morning, or by smiling.

Doing what's right may not always be the easiest route to take, but the results of doing the right thing produce good karma and help us to grow.

We all have at least one special hidden talent or gift. Most often, we don't even recognize our own talents (or self-worth). Each one of us is a gift to this beautiful life and each one of us contributes something unique to this beautiful life. Maybe each of us IS the gift to the universe and everything that we do is just icing on the cake in the eyes of the universe.

We all need to have goals. The problem arises that when we do not achieve our goals within the time frame that we think we should have achieved them, we tend to be quite harsh on ourselves. By setting smaller goals that we know can be achieved with relative ease we will begin to build our self-worth and be able to move on to accomplish larger and more challenging goals and accomplish THEM with relative ease. Works for me.

Everything, absolutely everything, is a part of the universe. We need to appreciate even the rain, storms-though they may not always be pleasant, they're part of the balance of life and are needed to complete the whole. Sunshine makes everything easier, the opposite of sunshine gives growth opportunities, not only to rebuild ourselves spiritually, but sometimes to rebuild our lives or to rebuild our environments.

"If you can't say anything nice about someone, don't say anything at all." Good advice. If we just take a second to think before we speak, we may realize that what we were going to say was unnecessary. By rethinking our words before we blurt them out, we can slowly change ourselves and become a kinder, gentler soul. Speak carefully. Think before you speak.

Being in love is incredible. It's a beautiful feeling. How about being in love all the time. Being in love with life, being in love with everyone, not romantically in love, but IN love. "In love" shouldn't always be romantic or sexual. I'm in love with everyone and everything -- I live my life IN love. Yes, I do walk around light headed and giggly most of the time, because I live in the love. Makes life much happier.

Solutions appear to us sometimes when we least expect them and from unexpected sources.

Taking life too seriously. We've all done it. We need to just BE in the moment. We fret, stress, worry about what "might" be. Instead of worrying about the coulda, shoulda, woulda situations of life, we must learn to live in the moment. The past is just that, it's over, done -- can't do anything at all about it. The future is not here yet – we cannot do anything about that either! What we have is right now, this very moment . . .

I recently found myself reacting to someone else's behavior in a way that was not me. At first, I couldn't understand my feeling of uneasiness. I did not like the person that emerged. I pulled back the reins and realized that this was not how I live my life. I run my life from my soul, not based upon what others do. I moved forward, being true to myself, and not basing MY actions upon someone else's actions.

Fear is a powerful controller, provided we let it be a powerful controller. Rather than let fear control us, perhaps turning our fears around into being gratitude rather than fear would take away the power of our fears. Living every second to the fullest, enjoying life, living from the pure love in our souls are all tools in overcoming fear.

Letting go of any given situation is not necessarily an innate part of our nature. It is a technique that must be learned. Once we understand that letting go and surrendering to the universe are techniques needed for us to live a more serene life, it becomes easier to let go of situations over which we have no control and to surrender totally regarding pretty much everything! The universe will provide what we need . . .

We look through windows. Are our eyes really the windows to our soul? I think they might be. Just like a window, we see the outside world using our eyes and people look within us by looking into our eyes. Just like a window.

Not one of us really, really knows what it is like to walk in someone else's shoes. We may have had similar experiences, but in reality, the only path on which we've walked is our own. Given the circumstances, I sometimes have to put blinders on to simply cope with whatever is occurring in my life at the time. Sometimes just moving forward, one baby step at a time, is a great challenge.

It's wonderful how people weave in and out of our lives throughout the years. Just when you think there is some stagnancy in life, all of a sudden, as if by wizardry, appears someone in your life with whom you connect on a marvelously deep, loving, soulful level. The universe is incredible. I am truly blessed with everyone in my life. Dear Universe, keep it coming!! Love, Jane

Isn't it wonderful that we all get to choose which direction we go on our own yellow brick road? Sure, the road goes in different directions, but ultimately, we all end up in the Emerald City. We have the choice as to which direction we wish to go. If we want something different, all we have to do is to change our direction. It really is that simple. It's all within.

While making my breakfast smoothie today I dropped the cranberries and they traveled all over the kitchen floor. My first inclination was to see if any kind of a pattern emerged, was there a hidden message that I was supposed to see within the cranberries? Nope. Don't think so. They were just all over the floor. Either that or I can't read cranberries.

Magic. It exists. Not necessarily in the form of a David Copperfield, but in the form of Mother Nature. Look at how perfectly the trees change color, go dormant, then turn so green. Watch the flowers. The bulbs know to appear magically in the spring followed by the summer flowers, then they go to sleep. Mother Nature provides us with the most perfect magic. Keep watching those sunrises and sunsets. Pure magic.

If I could only..." Well, I can. We all CAN. Simply by closing my eyes, I can travel from treetop to treetop, planet to planet, star to star, galaxy to galaxy. Everything is possible! Our human bodies are finite. Our imagination is infinite. I love living in the infinite, the possibilities are endless—I can be anything I want to be, do anything I want to do, travel anywhere I want to go. I love being limitless!!

When I exercise, I listen to rock & roll, while singing along at the top of my lungs. It's difficult to conceive of the fact that while screaming out this horrendous sound, the very same vocal cords are capable of singing a classical aria in any language! Made me realize that most of us don't grasp the concept of how versatile we truly are.

We don't have a fathom as to all of our abilities and capabilities.

The trick is not to take anyone or anything for granted. It's not necessarily so easy . . . We all tend to take our spouses for granted, our siblings, our children, our homes, the food we eat, our jobs, even our pets. I vote for an "I appreciate everything" day -- perhaps it should be every day. Maybe we all just need to be a little more aware...of everything. What do you think?

Part of what I like about myself is my creativity. In Jane's world, everything takes a positive turn. We all can create our own world. My name is Jane. I am an artist. I create. Who are you? What are you? What do you do?

It is so important to maintain our sense of humor. I'm grateful for my ability to laugh at pretty much anything at any time. I always find humor in any given situation. Though I do have to admit that humor is not necessarily appropriate all of the time-unbeknownst to anyone I'll almost always be chuckling about something in the back of my mind. Life is to enjoy – it makes no sense to take anything too seriously.

OK. So, the other day I had a case of the dropsies-everything I touched fell to the ground, much like the cranberries did the other morning- and distributed itself into some sort of random pattern. Well, you know me, I'm trying to read the mysterious patterns of everything, thinking that the universe had some deep, profound message for me. I came to the conclusion that I am just plain clumsy.

Interesting how certain people, whom we may have known for many years, are not really our friends. My true friends are those who are supportive of me, my endeavors and always showing me something positive or in a new light. My friends are kind, gentle and loving, and are able to show me new ways of looking at things. I hope that they perceive me as possessing those qualities regarding my friendship towards them.

Food, clothing and shelter -- the 3 basic needs of human beings. Not wants, but needs. There is a huge difference between the two. No matter what, my needs are always met. My wants, however...Well, they're always met too, just not necessarily in the time frame that I think "I want!"

Sometimes it's just time to move on, whether it be from a physical location or from people. Sometimes we must start anew. Not always easy. Losing my mother was a way in which I was not prepared to start anew, but was thrust into doing so. There are many ways to begin.

We all wear masks. If you have a headache and someone asks you how you're feeling, usually, you would say "fine.'" Or, if we're feeling a little under the weather for whatever reason, we usually say we're "fine." Why is it that we feel we must wear a "fine" mask when, in reality, we're not really fine? We've all done it.

Communicating with others can often be a challenge. We sometimes don't necessarily say what we mean and become frustrated when we don't receive the answers for which we're looking. If we take the attitude of "perhaps I did not express myself properly" and rephrase our words, frustrations will be dissipated.

Fast. Fast food. Driving fast. Not waiting on line in the supermarket. Everything has to be fast. We've forgotten to enjoy and appreciate life. All we want to do is to get through everything fast. It's a little sad, don't you think? For me, I do most things slow as a turtle and love every second of it. Gives me a deep appreciation for everything and I get the most out of each moment.

When we feel uncomfortable about someone or a particular situation, we must look within ourselves for the solution of what's really bothering us, and most of the time, we will find the answer within. This is how we bring about growth.

I took a Hula dance class and learned to Hula with the Hawaiian Christmas song, Mele Kalikimaka. Learning how to use your hands and arms as a form of expression was quite interesting, as every movement with your hands and arms in Hula dancing tells a part of a story. The next time I see dance from another culture, the movements, costuming and expressions will be seen in a different light.

When someone pushes our buttons, what's really going on inside of us? Having our buttons pushed can bring about feelings of annoyance, anger, frustration, etc.   If we could just learn to lighten up a little and laugh at ourselves, our buttons would no longer be pushed !

Perfection is measured in comparison with what we perceive something should be. If there is not another something of whatever it is to compare it to, doesn't that make the original something perfect in and of itself? I think so. Is there another you? Nope. Doesn't that make you perfect? Yup. Maybe none of us is perfect in everything we do, but in the large scheme of things, each of us is perfect in our own right.

One word for today: Unconditional. It can be followed by love, acceptance, gratitude, willingness--you fill in the blank. That one word, unconditional, is a doozey--it's a word that we have a tendency to put a condition upon. We need more "unconditional."

When reflecting on your accomplishments in life, look at everything in your past with gratitude. Every step you've taken and everything that's transpired in your life has brought you to where you are today and plays a part in your evolution.

There were an awful lot of penalties called in the football game this past weekend. Could you imagine if there were referees in life calling a penalty every time we did something that was a little out of bounds or incomplete? That sure would make life different! Do you think we would be more aware of what we were doing?

OK. So, I'm either the best sports fan in the world or the worst. Why? Because I am always happy for whatever team makes a good play (doesn't matter what sport), or I like a team because of the color of their uniforms (usually football).

Inspiration. I am often told that I inspire people. Not really sure how. But, I am happy to have a positive influence in life and to be an inspiration for people whose paths I have crossed. I am truly blessed.

I pray for peace often, not just on a global level, but that everyone may have the peace within themselves that will allow them to achieve a peaceful and loving way of living, and allow them to live life on a balanced keel.

I am grateful to be an artist, as self-expression comes easily to me. My emotions are emitted through song, music, painting, drawing, even knitting. For me, it is a challenge to find the proper words to express WHAT I'm feeling, not so much THAT I am feeling. Words (not that I am ever lacking) as an expression, are somewhat challenging to me.

Thoughts and Actions. An action always stems from a thought, but a thought remains just a thought until one takes action. It's kind of a good thing that not all thoughts are actions, don't you think?

Thank you for being the wonderful person that you are. I love you so very much. Great words to say to another person. Even better when you say them to yourself -- and mean it !!!

It's not what you say, but how you say it. Great saying, and rings true. Saying something to someone using the correct wording can make all the difference in the world. If we speak to someone with love, compassion and kindness, we diffuse potential attitudes of negativity. If we speak with sarcasm or "attitude," we can create dissention. Always best to opt for the loving route.

While riding the train home from Manhattan I was observing the skyline-beautiful clear blue sky-that is until you look and see the smog. Our air is horribly polluted. If each of us does something to make our environment better in whatever way, we can make a difference. After all, the whole is made of the sum of its parts. We are the parts of the universe. However tiny we are, each and every one of us is a part.

It's not so much that when change happens it happens suddenly, so much as it is that we don't necessarily notice the subtle changes that happen over a period of time. We seem to "grow" with them. When there's a sudden change, we notice it because we have not transitioned with it.

We all seek comfort and look for answers outside of ourselves. By looking for comfort and answers within, we grow and change. Seeking within is, in and of itself, the ultimate answer.

To err is human, to forgive-divine. We all make mistakes. We all do and/or say things we wish could be taken back. Sure, we can apologize, but ultimately, it is up to us as human beings to accept each other unconditionally. The forgiveness part – well, I don't think that's up to us . . . The universe seems to do a great job in keeping our karmic balance.

We all have our own time frame in accomplishing anything we do in life. Having patience to follow our path can be a challenge. Personally, I have to pull back the reins at times and understand that I may need more time to finish a task than I had originally thought. This helps me to understand that I can finish a task, not to become frustrated, and to work within my own time frame.

You exude whatever (however) it is that you are feeling at any given moment. If you feel happy, others will see you as a happy person. If you feel depressed or sad, others will see you as an unhappy person. You will be perceived as whatever you are feeling at any given time. Best to keep a smile on your face, don't you think? Even if you don't necessarily feel like smiling? It's that whole mask thing. . .

Is it really possible to love a particular someone or something more than the other? Isn't love just love? Maybe the objects of our affection can be loved differently, but I'm not so sure that anything or anyone can be loved more or less. Love is love is love is love . . . You either love, or you don't.

Healing Wounds. We cut a finger. Wash it. Put on a bandage. A scab forms. The scab falls off. The wound is healed. Maybe there's a scar, maybe not. How is that any different from an emotional wound? Emotionally, we plug through the same steps to heal inwardly, and sometimes there's a scar and sometimes not. When you think about it, time really does heal all wounds. Sometimes, we're left with a scar. . .

Are you a good witch or a bad witch?" "Well, I'm not a witch at all. Witches are old and ugly…" Interesting—our perception of things.

Interesting how we perceive others. For instance, if we see someone in a wheelchair or using a cane, we can see that they are disabled in some way. We grant that disabled person more courtesy. Why is that? Why can't we just grant everyone that same courtesy all of the time? Why do we put a condition upon our patience? Why should there have to be a perceived difficulty for us to be kinder or more courteous to someone?

I often think of how insignificant we really are-not even a grain of sand in the universe. Yet, we all are an important part of the whole scheme of everything. The whole of anything is a sum of its parts. Without even one part, the whole is no longer complete. So, each of us is important.

I have two rules: Never ski on weekends (too crowded with people who don't know what they're doing) and Never take the Cross Bronx Expressway (too crowded with people who don't know what they're doing). These are Jane's Rules. All rules are subject to being broken -- That's the rule of a rule!!! Oh, one other rule: Live every moment of life to the fullest. That rule is never broken. Oh – and my best rule of all, There Are No Rules.

A pebble thrown into the water produces ripples that go on forever. Those ripples don't stop when they reach land, only the ripples in the water cease, not the vibrations from ripples. The vibrations of the ripples continue forever on the land and keep going, ad infinitum. Any questions that everything we do has that same rippling effect in every phase of our lives? Vibrations. Life is built on vibrations.

Allowing oneself to feel whatever one is feeling at any given time creates a healthy inner environment. Even feeling fear is important. At least you are feeling something. We've all come across people who seem emotionless and without feelings. FEEL . . feel love, hate, fear, gratitude . . . but feel.

Tears. They're necessary sometimes. Tears are a release of emotion. A release of tension. A release of sadness. And sometimes, a release of joy. Crying is a healthy, normal reaction for us.

To fulfill one's destiny one must be true to oneself. Being true to yourself is just that, following your own destiny, creating your own karma, being your own person--Allowing yourself to follow your own path in life, in your own way. on your own schedule.

It is very easy for someone on the outside of a situation to make a judgment on how things should be done differently regarding someone else's life.

But we never truly know everything about another person's life until we are faced with that same type of situation. It is not for us to judge each other, but to be supportive towards each other. We never really know what is going on behind the scenes in someone else's life.

Today, it is my vow to take nothing seriously, to laugh at whatever I can--including myself--and to not take in any energy other than happy energy. Only love, laughter and happy energy are allowed into my life today.

Changing how we look at things can give us an entirely different perspective. Putting ourselves in someone else's shoes and trying to imagine their journey can give us insight and help us grow.

We have such a large capacity for love. Why are some people so afraid of love or being in love? It's so much easier to just let yourself feel the love for others that you feel. After all, we feel love unconditionally for children and animals. Why shouldn't that love be given unconditionally to everyone all of the time?

The birds outside are definitely chirping differently -- they know that spring is just around the corner. Animal behavior is amazing, don't you think? Their instincts are so sharp. Our instincts are sharp also, we just have to learn to listen to them!

I sometimes wonder how I would react if my cancer returned. The will to survive is strong. I probably would do whatever necessary to survive, just like the last two times.

Life is to enjoy, to live, to love -- not to fret and anguish over. Let's get out there and live, love and enjoy with gratitude -- for everything !!!!

Motivation. It's not always easy to stick to something, whether it be exercise, diet, plan of action – whatever. It becomes so much easier to follow through on things when we speak with someone else and become motivated, rather than relying on our own devices. We have to remember not to quit just before the miracle. I have to remember to follow my own advice.

Expectations. If we don't make an expectation about something, it is impossible to be disappointed. Yet we can still be elated at the outcome, it's only disappointment that is dissipated by not making an expectation, not joy.

There are those who need far more blessings, love and prayers than we can imagine. I'm blessed to know so many lovely light workers. Sending love and light to those in need is crucial to harmony and balance in the universe.

Wording. Do we always mean what we say? I've heard many people say things or ask questions while certainly meaning to say or ask something else. We need to be more aware and formulate sentences and questions using more descriptive wording. Choose your words wisely. Make sure that the question you're asking or what you're saying are the words with which you are properly expressing yourself.

What you put your focus upon is magnified. If your focus is on not having time to do things, you will not have the time to do things. If you focus on living life in love and gratitude, amazing miracles continuously enter your realm. Do you want to focus on not being able to do things in your life or to have abundance of everything wonderful. My choice is the latter . . .

I recently watched the move "The Yes Man." What would life be like if we all approached every day with a yes (or even a maybe) rather than a "oh, no, I can't do THAT" for whatever silly reason we think is valid at the time? Don't you think it's worth a conscious effort to be open to the possibility of something?

Maybe. Interesting word. It gives one hope…it's a "perhaps." We should always have hope. No one has the right to take away our hope.

Having enthusiasm and passion are similar, in fact, I'm not really sure of what the difference between the two would be. If you're enthusiastic about something, you have a passion for it, and vice versa. Any thoughts?

My father's roommate died an hour ago. I was there and had the chance to perform one of the most ministerial duties I will ever do -- I was able to bless him upon his passing to the other side. My father and I then discussed how similar birth and death really are. In both cases, one second you're here, and the next second, you're not here.

Faith. Trust. Belief. Love. Hope. Common Sense. If we do our best to incorporate all of these qualities in each moment of every day, our lives will be enriched.

I often feel as if I have my invisibility cloak on when I'm in a crowd – as if no one can see me. I've felt this way while others whom I know have conversed around me and I have been left out of a conversation, as if I were invisible.

Learning. I find it wonderful to be a blank canvas every day so that the universe can devise a lesson plan for me and paint its beautiful pictures through my mind and my eyes.

It is really incredible to me that on the days that I think I have nothing substantial to say, I receive the most comments. My mother always said that doing or saying nothing is still doing or saying something, and sometimes it is best to say or do nothing. I continue to learn from my mother's words of wisdom.

If we keep hitting road blocks in what we're doing in life, perhaps we need to step back and reevaluate our course. Often what's needed is to change an attitude, or how we're going about doing something. Nothing in life that we're pursuing should be quite that tough. Life is a great process to be cherished every inch of the way. It should be enjoyed with gratitude.

On days when I'm feeling overwhelmed, it is important that I take a deep breath, slow down a little and BE 100% in the moment. By focusing on each task at hand I am able to plug through the day with a feeling of accomplishment.

We are all on this earthly plane on a journey. We are spirit living within a physical, human body. Some people will never understand or get that during this lifetime. We cannot necessarily topple on over to another dimension by will to just be our spiritual essence, at least not until we cross over to the other side at the finish of our life cycle – or sometimes through meditation we can visit another dimension, but being that we are human, finite beings living an earthly existence, we cannot stay in that place of a different dimension. We can, consciously, as much as humanly possible, develop our spirit essence to enable us to live in light and love.

Did you ever remove the garbage from your kitchen garbage pail and place the filled bag on the kitchen chair or on the floor without having tied it up, and during that split second that you stepped away, as if my some practical joke played on you by the universe, the bag topples over and your garbage, which up until just a moment ago was neatly in its bag, is all over your floor? Glad to know it's not just me.

You hold a door for someone while leaving a store, or the post office, or wherever, and there is another door through which you must go. The person for whom you held the door now holds the outer door for you (or vice versa). This is instant karma. Think about other places in your life where instant karma occurs.

Problems often seem insurmountable, larger than life, yet we get through them and they soon become a memory. But at the time we're in the middle of them, they're often tough. Perhaps if we didn't give our challenges that much energy in the first place, they would be easier to move through. What do you think?

Anxiety sometimes gets the better of me. It is important to breathe--just breathe deeply and know that I will get through whatever it is that weighs so heavily on my mind. All of life's moments are so fleeting, both the good moments and the challenging ones.

When we learn to let go of things beyond our control, life becomes much easier. And, most things are beyond our control!! We can hold on to something and try to control it, or we can let it go and understand that the universe had a divine plan for us and enjoy the ride! It's all in our attitude.

The power of example is the greatest teacher. We can always learn by observing others. Sometimes we learn what to do and sometimes what not to do, but we can always learn something from the examples of others.

Often in life we're given a second chance. I try to use that second chance as a learning experience. Obviously, during my "first chance," I did not do all that well. I do my best to use my second chance as a new jumping off point and to learn as much as I can.

I don't live in fear, but I do sometimes experience
the feelings associated with it. I hate that feeling of
"oh my god, what's going to happen next." I hate
to say "hate." Fear is so crippling & anxiety
producing. When I can pull myself together & live
in the love & gratitude that is usual for me, I feel
much better.

When we feel anger or any other emotion that is
less than positive, the only way to rid ourselves of
that particular emotion is to change from within. It
is only when we feel those negative emotions that
we realize we need to change.

All of us feel insecure at times, we don't know
what to do, say or how to act sometimes. It helps
to remember that we are never alone in these
feelings. Absolutely everyone feels these
challenges. It may seem as if someone is having
an easy time of things, but we can't see their
insides. They're the same as ours.

Learning to embrace that which we fear or what
makes us feel uncomfortable, dissipates that fear
and sense of discomfort. When we practice this
regularly, we are able to live our lives in harmony
and have inner peace.

I saw a female swan sitting on her nest yesterday.
As she was sitting on the nest, she was picking up
pieces of nesting materials and building the nest
around her. Amazing. Truly amazing.

Memories. Our lives are built on memories. We
learn from memory, by repetition of things, which
is the same as having "remembered" things.

Everything we know is from memory—whether it be stories handed down ("his-story"), patterns we learn to repeat. We need to create new memories to in order to learn and move forward.

Wind. We can't see wind, only the results of wind. How many other things are there that we can't see? Why do people think that they have to be able to see something to know it's there? Just because it is unseen doesn't mean that it doesn't exist . . .

Do you see that line above? I don't know why it's there. I can't get rid of it. Tried everything. So, what's the lesson here? Acceptance? I can't change it, so it would seem that acceptance is my lesson. That can be a challenging lesson when you have your mind set on something else!

On line at the store, there was a bag of Fritos someone must have discarded which was at the end of the counter. The woman behind me asked if the bag of Fritos was mine. My mind began saying "what, are you kidding? I don't eat that stuff." But instead of reacting, I stopped myself and said "No, it isn't. Thank you though." It's all in the attitude.

I know nothing. A plethora of nothing. Knowing nothing allows me to be open to be able to learn something. Way cool.

Something to think about: When pig farmers feed their pigs raw potatoes, the pigs stay slender. Since farmers sell their pigs by the pound, they have learned to feed them cooked potatoes, which fattens them up. Glad I'm raw vegan. I wouldn't sell for much in the by the pound market !!

When we have an opportunity to do something, we should grab it when it is in front of us. If we don't take advantage of opportunities as they're presented, they are usually gone forever and can lead to regret, or what I call the "shoulda, woulda, couldas." In order to live life to the fullest, use each opportunity as it presents itself. Trying & Doing. There is a big difference between trying and doing. We can try forever, but when you DO something, you get results. You can either spend your life trying, or just do it!!! (Wish I had thought of that as a slogan for a popular sports brand.)

The body needs nutrition, like a car needs gas (or electricity, or whatever it needs to run nowadays). We are living this life on loan from The Universe, and we need to take care of ourselves. Not having had my health for so long, I am now committed to living my life to the fullest and healthiest extent possible.

There's that line again. OK. Not just acceptance, but making the best or the most of any given situation, even when it's not what you'd planned.

Meditation. Daily meditation maintains my serenity. It keeps me living in gratitude. It allows me to be my true self and keeps me focused on assisting others when necessary and living in love.

Intention. If you have good intentions, you're probably moving in the right direction even if things don't pan out the way you anticipated. If your intent is not pure, watch out . . . karma can be tricky.

Transformation, metamorphosis, it all boils down to change. But being that we are creatures of habit and find change a little taxing sometimes, maybe it's easier to substitute a different word for change . . . alteration, variation, shift, variety. A little mind trick to play on yourself.

Exclusion. Remember in grade school how icky it felt to be excluded from anything? As adults, we occasionally still feel left out of things. It kind of stirs up those old childhood feelings, doesn't it? Let's keep in mind how good it feels to be included and make a conscious effort to take the time to include others in our lives.

Sometimes, a quick nap or a brief meditation is all that is necessary to renew the spirit. It can be only a few moments . . . Remember that you can begin your day over again at any point during the day!

Granting each other common courtesies should be second nature. We should not even have to think about respecting each other or being kind, yet everything is so fast and so busy, we sometimes take life for granted at the expense of each other.

When I visited with my father today, I watched him struggle with this gadget to help him button his shirt. It's a wire that slips through the buttonhole, then grabs the button and pulls it through the buttonhole. It took him several minutes to button four buttons. Made me think of how much I take many things for granted – something so simple as my ability to use my fingers to slide a button through a button hole.

Keeping the buzz of life going doesn't mean that you are hanging around bees! It simply means that you are living in the excitement of the now of life.

I had a dream last night that Arnold Schwarzenegger bought me a baby parakeet. I'm usually pretty good with dream interpretations, but this one has me stymied. Any thoughts? Oh, and the other night, Glenn (my husband) thought I was walking on the ceiling (in his sleep of course).

Why do we think we need reasons for things? If we love and accept unconditionally, reasons become unnecessary. Reason, justification, the "whys" of life don't really matter if we are living life with unconditional love and acceptance.

Have you ever had anyone burst your bubble when you've been happy or oh so enthusiastic about something? Not fun, is it. It can be a huge emotional crash. I do my best to be encouraging to someone when they're enthused; compassionate when they're sad; and to say spiritually comforting words when necessary. I always strive to allow someone to stay in their happy bubble, but do my best to lure them out of their sad bubble.

It is not the destination, it is the journey. The journey just keeps on getting better and better!!! I am so blessed to be living this glorious life, even with all of its challenges.

Today I will act how I want to see the world. I want to see more love in the world, so I will act in love. I want to see more kindness in the world, so I will act in kindness. You get the picture.

When we choose to be accepting of life's incredible gifts, it becomes astounding at how abundantly they are given to us.

Awakening our hearts and souls to the joy of life doesn't take much but a conscious effort to dance to the heart beat of the universe.

We are not in control of most things. The only thing over which I know that I have control is my attitude. Today I will be positive. There. It's simple.

I don't quite understand why people are so quick to make judgments about other people or situations rather than accepting their differences with others: accepting and loving unconditionally. Putting conditions on life's circumstances is the same as making a judgment that things should be and have to be a certain way. I've heard it said that "there are many ways to skin a cat." Though I don't particularly like that phrase, the meaning is clear: We are all different in our thoughts and actions, with the same end result. Each of us is different. That's all.

"Sweet dreams till sunbeams find you. Sweet dreams that leave your worries behind you. But in your dreams, whatever they be, dream a little dream of me." Ever wonder who thinks about you? and when? or why?

It's interesting how you can look at a thousand photos of someone and not know them. All it takes is one "in person" encounter, and ZAP, you know them.

Have you ever had anyone burst your bubble when you've been happy or oh so enthusiastic about something? Not fun, is it. It can be a huge emotional crash. I do my best to be encouraging to someone when they're enthused; compassionate when they're sad; and to say spiritually comforting words when necessary. I always strive to allow someone to stay in their happy bubble, but do my best to lure them out of their sad bubble.

Is "if" such a challenging word? I don't know. Perhaps substituting "if' with another word or a different phrase may help in processing something that has the word "if" in it. Rephrasing makes a great difference in our perception and can aid us in the true meaning of the words being spoken (or written!).

Though I find it somewhat unnerving, when I'm around certain people (especially some from my past), I find myself slipping into behavioral patterns that I didn't think were part of me anymore. As long as I'm aware of this situation, I have the ability to change it when it happens.

While our intentions may be good, until we follow through with them, they are meaningless. Action is required. Otherwise, intentions are just thoughts.

Patience is not just something to be shown to others. We must have patience with ourselves as well. When we are patient and loving towards ourselves, it becomes easier to be patient and loving towards others. Patience, kindness, loving – all similar.

Yin/yang, heads/tails, life/death, happiness/sadness, love/hate-all the same coin, different sides; all closely interwoven with fine lines separating them.

When you find yourself in a situation or with a person that triggers something from your past causing actions or reactions that are not typical of how you are now, how do you deal with those unexpected emotions? A trigger can cause our behavior to be different; suddenly our emotions and actions are not our own.

You never truly know whose life you touch or how -- whether it be with a smile, or a compliment, or a "good morning." You just never know . . .

Tip of the day: Gardening is good for the soul. There's something that makes you feel so good while digging in the dirt, even if it's just for a few moments. The real tip is, don't wear good shoes while gardening, even if you think you're just going to be out there briefly. Shoes will get filled with dirt and mud no matter how careful you think you're going to be! I speak from experience.

As adults, it is up to us to show young ones, through our behavior, how one should act in any given situation. It is up to us to be adults; to keep our word, to act like grown-ups. If we fail to do this, we will be creating confused children, who grow up to be confused adults.

I recently had a "happenstance" which left me feeling insignificant, sad, neglected, left out, and just plain hurt. After a while of crying and letting my emotions run their course, with a change of attitude, all I needed to do was think about what I have, and choose to have an attitude of gratitude towards everything in my life. We can learn something from everything if we are open to the experience.

Very rarely is any challenge caused by outside sources. When we look within, we will find solutions -- always -- and realize that most of our challenges are of our own making !! It's our attitude that provides us with a solution. If we look upon things with a positive attitude, our experiences will be positive. It's always our own attitude . . .

What is obvious to one is oblivious to another. We need to keep in mind that not everyone thinks the same way we do. Patience and kindness are important to practice when dealing with what we perceive to be the obvious!

Laughter is exercise for the soul.

Today my father was talking about his needs "when he gets home." Though I outwardly agree with him and say "OK, that can be done," I know that he's not going to be coming home. He needs care 24/7, well, maybe not care so much as supervision, which would be impossible for him to receive if he were living here. He also has a good degree of socialization in the nursing home, which he also would not have here. After all, I don't provide ice cream socials on the patio every Thursday!

Acceptance and forgiveness. They are so very similar. If you've accepted, you've forgiven. If you've forgiven, well, sometimes you've accepted! With acceptance, everything else that's good follows.

Having a gratitude attack sure feels a lot better than having a panic attack!! I choose to live in love and gratitude. It IS a choice !!!

Isn't it amazing how the butterflies know that the butterfly bushes are there just for them. They have keen instincts for an insect. Our instincts are keen as well. We just have to trust them and follow them !

Doing everything, speaking, eating, exercising -- with proper intent is healthy. When speaking, choose your words and speak with intent. When eating, eat with intent that the food will provide your body with nutrition. When you exercise, exercise with intent that your body is becoming healthier. Intent makes a difference. Try it for just a day and see how much better you feel.

Love and Fear. If you are fearful, you need to fill yourself with love. Fear cannot exist while you are living in love. By the same token, love does not exist while you are living in fear. I choose to live in love. It is a choice I make to live in love and gratitude.

It's rainy. Thunder and lightning. No sunshine. I found myself slipping into a little bit of a depression. When I realized this, I quickly changed my thoughts to gratitude. When I filled myself with gratitude, the depression had no place to live within me. Gratitude. Love and Gratitude.

Having good health is a choice. Trouble is, we almost always wait until something catastrophic has happened to us to CHOOSE to take whatever steps are necessary for us to achieve and maintain good health. Wouldn't it be great to live in a world where the fast food would be organic romaine lettuce wraps filled with living hummus or guacamole? And our super sized beverages would be green tea or spring water with lemon, orange and lime slices?

Many of us are so busy taking care of other people and things that we sometimes forget to take care of ourselves. Today, I will be loving and gentle toward me. I will treat my body with the respect it deserves and feed it properly with live, living food. I will nourish my soul with loving thoughts of love and gratitude.

We often perceive that we do not have time in our lives. We have as much time as we want to have to do whatever we'd like to do, so long as it's a priority. If we don't want to do something, we shouldn't say that we don't have "time" to do it, we should be honest and say that it's not a priority for us to do.

July 19th was my mother's birthday. She would be in her mid 90s now, but instead, because she neglected to take care of herself, she died at 75 years of age. She taught me one of the most valuable lessons I could ever have learned--to take care of my physical body. Thank you Florie for teaching me that. You have influenced my life beyond your wildest imagination.

As humans, we have free will. In exercising that free will, many do not realize that they have a choice to be happy, sad, healthy, etc. Once that is realized, and a person exercises their free will to adjust their attitude, life becomes blessed. That which was perceived as a problem, no longer exists as a problem, and we begin to magically partake in the journey of life.

Making changes within ourselves can be challenging. We often make unrealistic expectations of ourselves and when we are unable to manifest those grand changes, our behavior becomes self-defeating. If we set smaller goals for ourselves that we can achieve, we will begin to build our self-esteem, leading the way to making changes within ourselves.

Being a non-denominational minister, I do not subscribe to any one particular religion or belief system. To me, all religions have wonderful aspects to them. What a person is made from, however, is a strong foundation of faith and spirituality, very different from a structured religious belief system. If everyone lived their life in love and gratitude, the world would be a happier place for all.

As a minister, it brings me great joy to marry those who are in love and wish to spend their lives together. It does not make a difference to me who they are insofar as religion, color, sex or whatever other differences may be perceived, just as long as the two people whom I marry are in love with each other. Love is beautiful and should be respected for what is is, Love. No one should have the right to tell any two people in love that they can or cannot be married. This whole country needs to step it up a bit and change with the times. Love is love.

As finite beings, it's next to impossible for a human to understand infinity and to accept things that cannot be logically explained. The god or divine deity is that part of many us is within our soul, not an outside source of human-created grandiosity. Some people choose to call it god, I prefer to call it Universe, as I feel that is the source of all energy, the universe, and we are fortunate enough to tap into that vast source of energy.

Anger. When I feel anger, I allow it to be there ever so briefly, then I let it go and thank the Universe for giving me this challenge (whatever it may be) and send the anger away with love, blessings and gratitude, or I bless the other person involved and send them love. That's what I do with anger.

I am deeply honored to live this beautiful life. It is a gift beyond my wildest expectations and dreams.

Every second is a blessing and each day a bonus. I am honored that the Universe has given me the ability to live my life in the beauty of love and gratitude.

Detachment can sometimes be tough. Like when you have a great idea for someone that you know, in your heart of hearts, fits them, but they are not interested. The challenge is to keep in mind that everyone is on a different path, and their path is NOT your path! We sometimes need to just detach from the situation and let it go with blessings. We all find our own way.

Arguing. Someone did their best today to have an argument with me. It was impossible, because it takes two people to argue and I was not a candidate. They kept pushing and pushing, and I just kept saying thank you, perhaps I was mistaken, thank you for pointing that out to me. This continued for several minutes until I finally smiled and walked in another direction. Peoples' perceptions of things are interesting. What she perceived to be important (arguing, perhaps being "right", whatever else) and what I perceived to be important, were different.

If we can remember not to take things personally, and that most things in life are NOT about us, we will be at peace within ourselves. It's when we start to think that they DID something to ME or why did that happen, or how could they do this, that we run into problems.

Life is so fleeting. Everything is temporary. Why do we let ourselves get so caught up in the meaningless nonsense?

Laughter – having a sense of humor is oh so very important. Even in the midst of what may seem to be something tragic or not "funny" at all – we still must "always look at the bright side of life." One of Monty Python's better ideas . . .

You gain knowledge from experience, but you do not gain experience from knowledge.

Interesting how self-absorbed some people can be. They say they're busy and they can't talk to you right now, not taking into consideration that you may be the one who needs to talk. Human nature is interesting.

While walking in NYC or taking a subway, I've often wondered why people always say hello to me. Without fail. Ok, so I'm usually smiling, and I always respond happily. But why do people take that initiative to speak in a city that is known for its fast pace and rudeness? Yes, NY is fast-paced, but I'm not sure from where it's gotten the rude reputation.

We must be grateful for the rain as well as the sunshine. Mother nature has given us a balance, and for that balance, we must be grateful. When mother nature gets angry with us for mistreating our earth, she lets us know. Give joy for today. Be in the moment. Love and appreciate this beautiful home we call earth.

Opportunity. When you have the opportunity to do something, better take that opportunity when it's presented. If you think about it for too long, or wait for another chance, that opportunity will have been long gone by the time you think you're ready to have taken it. My father taught me this a long time ago.

It's only when we make expectations on others that we think we need the power to forgive...forgiveness of any perceived wrongdoings on our part comes from sources much higher than humans. There is no need for forgiveness if we live in unconditional love and acceptance, without making expectations on others, loving and accepting them for who they are, what they do--just loving them...

While overhearing two strangers' conversations, I was able to assist in a question to which neither knew the answer. Though I don't recommend eavesdropping, there are occasions here and there when it is of help to someone and has its merits. As with anything, when used for the wrong reasons, it's not so good.

I am Grateful that I'm here for people to talk to. I must be doing something right, as they come freely to me and speak openly when they ordinarily would not speak freely. Providing a safe place for people to express themselves is important, as we all need an outlet.
Our selfishness as human beings is sometimes astounding. We do or don't do things because we want to or don't want to do them rarely thinking of the impact we may have on others, that whatever

it is that we do may help someone else, even if we "don't feel like doing it" or we think we haven't a need to do something. The next time you don't think you want or need to do something, do it anyhow. Your presence may be of help to someone, or you may say something profound to another.

When we say something positive, the vibrations from that stay with us and emanate from us all through the day.

Stinkin' Thinkin'. I'm going to steer clear of my own thoughts today and let the Universe fill me with beautiful thoughts of love, gratitude, joy and laughter. When left to my own devices, my thoughts can put me in an uncomfortable place.

Life is a series of choices. The results are what you get based upon your choices. Choose wisely and carefully, with intent !!!

It has been my observation that some people are in "control mode" and have forgotten to practice acceptance with dignity and grace. They want things their way or no way. Saying thank you and accepting the circumstance with dignity and grace seems the better route. Think about your actions and your reactions to others. Handle situations with grace (gratitude) while maintaining your personal self-esteem.

Remember that you don't always have to be right about things. Sometimes we just need to let things go and not hold on with our ego. That there can always be value in what someone says, even if you don't agree with it. Everyone has the right to their feelings, emotions and opinions. Thank the person for sharing their views and move on. This will help you to live within yourself peacefully. It really does work.

Even a small adjustment in one's attitude can change a life-challenging situation into a tiny speed bump in life. Just a small attitude adjustment . . .

I am a beautiful person. I have a wonderful energy, giving love and joy to everyone I meet. I am grateful for the lessons in my life, because all of my lessons build my strength of character. I live my life accepting of others, always being non-judgmental. I live my life loving others unconditionally. I live my life in gratitude for everything and everyone in my life. That's what helps _me_ get through the day.

Affirmations are a wonderful resource to use to build your self-esteem. Look in the mirror this morning and really LOOK at the person you see. Tell that person they are wonderful and you are blessed to know them. Carry that around with you throughout the day and I'll bet you will feel great all day long!!! Remember to use positive affirmations.

We all are subject to life's annoyances. When I find myself getting steamed about something, I make a conscious effort to send love to it – whether it be a person or a situation, or whatever. I just send love. That helps to keep my side of the street clean, so to speak, and keeps a healthy karma going. When in doubt, pull back the reins and send love. Also, acceptance plays a part as does the ability to laugh!!

Sometimes it's best to keep on smiling even if you don't feel like it. Sometimes acting "as if" you are happy can actually create joy and happiness, and help you to forget about your not-so-happy feelings. Acting "as if" can help in many circumstances.

Do you ever feel like you're stuck? When that happens, take action to un-stick. Move forward somehow, first in thought and then in action. Even the smallest of actions can un-stick you in your life and allow your energy to flow and help to bring you into the moment and able to move into the future.

Unconditional acceptance makes such a huge difference in my life. When my car broke down the other day, I kind of chuckled and just said "OK, Universe, I don't know what you have in store for me, but thank you for keeping me safe. Thank you for the tow truck that magically appeared behind me. Thank you for making my life interesting." And I moved on to whatever was next. I am grateful. Sure, my car broke down, but there was this tow truck that just appeared. Took me to a place to get my new transmission. Just one of life's little speed bumps.

I think we all know that every action begins with a thought and that not all thoughts (thankfully!) become actions. I do my best to let the good thoughts flow and to act upon them, and to dismiss the not so good ones. I suppose that would be the difference between sanity and insanity!

Decisions. Making a decision is great, but is meaningless without taking action on that decision. We all know – 3 frogs on a log, one decided to jump off, how many frogs are left . . . 3, one decided to jump off. No action, only a decision. So you see, we must take action on our decisions in order to move forward. Or we can just sit and ponder our decision to pieces as to whether or not we've made the right decision, or if we should make a different decision, never taking any action, only to remain totally stagnant, sitting in wonderment as to why our life is so horrendously boring (that's my New York sarcasm still kicking around). It is important to take action on your decision. Any action is moving forward.

I prefer to use the word "challenge" rather than problem or trouble. For me, if I look at things as a challenge, I become motivated to move through it, over it, past it, and progress. If I think of something as an obstacle, I find it difficult to move past that obstacle. The word challenge creates motivation for me.

Each of us has a special quality that we bring to the Universe, actually, that the Universe has bestowed upon us! When we open ourselves up to sharing that special quality, whatever it may be, life has a certain flow, as that is when we are being true to ourselves.

Pushing ourselves to experience things outside of our comfort zone is important to our character building. If we always stay within our comfort zone, we never grow. When we give that extra little push to do something unfamiliar and unknown, we develop inner strength and broaden our horizons.

Each of us has the option of taking action to change situations in our lives. Sometimes taking action means that we do something physically to change a situation. Sometimes it is a spiritual change or a change in our own attitude. Whatever the action is that we take doesn't really matter just so long as we take action and move forward.

Winter is upon us. The Winter Goddess enfolds us with the love of her icy embrace. She reminds us of the purity of our souls by giving us virgin snow. She reminds us of life's frailty by giving us ice, showing us how something so beautiful can be equally as destructive, teaching us to exercise moderation in our lives. Proceed with heightened awareness in the ice and snow and the Winter Goddess will engulf you with her love and protection.

Many of us are quick to make a judgment of someone or a circumstance based upon our perception, not necessarily knowing all the facts involved. It's amazing to me that we put conditions on things. I find that if I love and accept unconditionally, I have no need to make judgments, only to send love and blessings.

If you remove your thought that you are unable to do something, what you're left with is the ability to do anything.

When we harbor a resentment, we are giving that resentment power -- whether it be toward a situation or a person. Think about it. Do you want to empower the resentment or do you want to be the one who is empowered? Awareness, together with a shift in attitude, will diminish the power of the resentment and empower you.

We see a difference in a baby 7 months old and a young person 7 years old; again a difference 14 years old; a difference 21 years old. Somewhere between about 30 and 50 we don't see that much of a difference. As we start to get older, from maybe 55-60 and up, those changes (about every 7 years) again, become more pronounced, as they were when we were younger. Just because we are adults and we don't necessarily see the physical changes as much as we used to, doesn't mean we aren't changing.

On the news this morning they said that January 17th is the most depressing day of the year. Let's all keep our heads above water on January 17th, and know that the Universe has a divine plan for us all and we're on it. Challenges occur, but we always work through them and become that much better in the long run. Blessings everyone.

We never know what someone else is going through. They may appear to us to be happy, while on the inside, they are suffering. We don't know someone's personal challenges or their day-to-day situations. We only see the outside. Let's all try to be more loving towards and accepting of others with the understanding that they may be going through their own "stuff" and may need others to treat them with some love & compassion.

I live in love and gratitude. When I say thank you enough, there is no fear, no anxiety, my mind doesn't race, it keeps me centered and knowing that I'm not in control. There is a far greater plan than I could imagine and I know that the Universe is keeping me on that divine plan!

You can either spend an exorbitant amount of energy simply "trying" to do something or you can just do it! If you keep trying, you can only do that, try, never achieving the goal.

We rely on our memory in order 2 learn in a repetitive fashion. Sometimes we must let go of what we remember in order 2 move past blockages. We may remember someone from our past as being a bully who might have grown 2 be the kindest person we could possibly know. We all change. Our perception of things must change as well. Sometimes letting go of old ideas (memories) will assist us in moving forward and letting go of our obstacles.

Relax the throat. Sing on the vowels. Use the diaphragm for support. Open the back of the throat. Relax the shoulders. Open your mouth. Don't worry about how you look (not easy). Let the voice flow. Don't let the microphone intimidate you, it is your friend. Just sing out. I still have to remind myself of all of this every time I sing. Except for when I'm in the shower.

The next time you find yourself becoming agitated with someone or something, pull back your reins a bit and try to understand where that agitation is coming from. Take a deep breath, and change your attitude!!! Remember -- everyone is on their own path in life, it's different from your path, but it's theirs. Be loving, patient and accepting of others . . .

Spring: The dance of the spring fairies brings forth nature's unforeseen beauty. They've sprinkled their magic fairy dust for the trees to bud, the flowers to blossom & the birds to nest. Their magical presence brings us together in the wonderment of love . . . Ahhhh . . . Spring . . .

Blessings come to us in many forms, some of which are not always pleasant at the moment they're occurring. It's important to understand that the Universe brings us everything we need in order to grow and to evolve into the best person we can become.

All it takes is a small shift in your attitude in order to have a wonderful day. Remember to live in love and gratitude. Be conscious of that.

Amazing how we can hold on to something from our past and allow it to influence us so much in the present. Learning to let go is often quite a challenge, but once we do let go of our past baggage, it is very freeing.

While sitting in the dentist's office the other day, I realized that the person behind the desk who answers the phone and deals with the patients is constantly being tested. Patience, tolerance and acceptance all play a huge role in that type of job. Not to mention the lessons in letting go and not getting involved with other people's stuff !!! It's not an easy job to deal with people day in and day out . . .

Let's all try to keep in mind that much can be misconstrued in e-mails. Realize that what you've written may be clear in your mind, but when someone else reads your words, what you've written may be interpreted differently in their mind.

Last night as I tossed and turned and was unable to fall asleep, I realized that I was living outside of my usual place of love and gratitude. I immediately pulled back the reins and focused on being grateful for everything, drifting off into a peaceful night's rest. Amazing what a little change in attitude can do!!!

Have you noticed that we judge others based upon what we are, how we think, and what our life experience has been? Being that I am aware of that, I want to be able to accept with unconditional love rather than to judge. We all have a path to follow, and I shouldn't be judgmental of another's path, as they should not judge mine. I will accept others with love.

A decision is just that -- a decision. Unless we take action on that decision, the decision remains in our minds. We have the ability to take action . . . to change our lives. Today, I will act on my decisions and move forward in my life.

When we like or dislike something about
someone, often it is a reflection of something
within ourselves that we like or strive to be like, or
a quality that we dislike about ourselves and we
need to change. Either way, we should learn from
the experience of our feelings, whether they be
feelings of admiration, like, discomfort, dislike --
you get the picture!

Prayers are thoughts. All action is based upon a
thought. Prayers become action. Think about it.

It's easy to have faith when things are going well,
it's taken for granted, it's just there. It's more
challenging put that faith into action in the face of
adversity. That's when our faith is put to the test!
Remember to have faith that this too shall pass,
there is a light at the end of the tunnel--everything
changes. . .constantly. . . keep the faith. . .The sun
is still there, even though, right now, it's behind the
clouds.

People and situations come into our lives not to
annoy us (although it may sometimes seem that
way!) but rather to help us grow. It is through the
gift of others and challenging situations that we
can begin to change what we need to change from
within.

Starting out with smaller goals and achieving
those smaller goals allows you to begin focusing
your effort towards a grander mission in life. We
may not always know what our ultimate mission is,
but we are on our journey to get there, and by
accomplishing smaller goals, we gain confidence

to move forward, allowing those seemingly "out of reach" goals to become within our reach.

Making a choice to do something or not to do something is prioritizing. When we prioritize, we are putting our life in the order in which we want it to be. Make your choices wisely and be aware that your choice is a priority.

Before saying something, think carefully -- what is the purpose of what you want to say? Will there be any repercussions from your words? Will your words be hurtful, or constructive? Can you rephrase your words into something more positive? Be aware of your intent when you speak. Blessings

Change is the only thing in life that's permanent.

Being true to yourself has only one meaning, and it is up to you to figure out what it means for you and to follow it. Your inner truths do not belong to someone else. Following your inner truths is what keeps you on your path in life.

Have faith that you are being guided and that you are on the correct path in life for you -- whatever that path may be. Having faith sometimes goes hand in hand with having patience -- patience to know that everything unfolds exactly as it is supposed to unfold -- not necessarily in YOUR time, but in the eyes and time of the Universe. Have faith and patience.

I'm often asked how one goes about changing their behavior. Well, one way is to first be aware of how you react to something and rather than letting that first reaction out, think for a moment on how you would like to appear differently to the outside world. Think about your response, choose a more loving approach, and then let yourself react within that love and how you wish to be perceived.

Interesting when you have a lot, you always have people around you wanting what you have. But when you have little, there are not always people around you wanting to help you. Just an observation.

There's a song that the Rolling Stones did, You Can't Always Get What You Want. I have come to the realization that you ALWAYS get what you want, it's just that you may not get it when you think you want it and it may be in a different form than you thought you had asked for. Moral of the story -- be really specific when you ask the Universe for something, as you will always get exactly what you asked for.

We are creatures of habit and tend to like things to always be status quo. When situations bring us outside of our comfort zone, it is time for a change – whatever that change may be, it's the Universe giving us a gentle nudge (or maybe not so gentle!) to move on and do something different and to grow.

Compassion. Having understanding and love for others can be challenging. By practicing unconditional acceptance and love towards others, we can develop compassion. By utilizing that compassion, we become kinder and more accepting of everything. Having compassion towards others is a healthy practice, helps us to grow and to become a kinder person.

The sun is still shining, even though it's raining. For days. I know the sun is up there cause I saw it once above the clouds & rain when I was in a plane. Really I did. I know it's there. I suppose that's faith.

We are all students & teachers. We all must listen to our students & teachers. It may not always be easy to listen & to hear, but we can always learn. I am consistently amazed as to where and how lessons are learned in life. I am truly grateful for all the lessons that I continually learn and pray that I will always be open for new experiences and new lessons in my life. Often, we can learn by the actions of others. Sometimes we want to be like another, and sometimes we want anything but to be like another. Both are lessons.

I prefer to use the word challenge rather than obstacle or blockage. Either way, they're nothing more than speed bumps in life. We have them before us, we work through them, we emerge on the other side of them, being that much stronger a person for having worked our way through our challenge(s). Today, I will graciously accept all that the Universe sets forth before me, knowing that the Universe has far greater plans for me than I could ever imagine.

When we are in conflict about something, the most effective way of handling any situation is to pray for a harmonious outcome.

It's a cloudy day today, but I know that above the clouds, there is blue sky and sunshine. You know -- every cloud has a silver lining, so to speak.

The angels of the autumnal equinox are present. They are bringing us our beautiful colors of the fall. They are jumping and playing in the fallen leaves. They are lovingly putting the trees to bed for their winter's sleep. They are blessing us with the cool, crisp fall air and beautiful bright blue sky of autumn.

Fantasies are usually better than reality.

I can think of a small handful of regrets that I have. All of them involve things that I did not do. None of them involve what I have done. I say, live -- follow your heart's desires -- live life to the fullest and be happy . . . That's what I say . . .

Happiness comes from within. Once you have found happiness within your soul, you realize how fleeting the moments of petty annoyances are and everything surrounding you becomes an experience filled with love, gratitude and joy -- even those moments we find to be most challenging!!!

I've recently had the opportunity to extend myself far beyond my normal comfort zone. There was some fear involved, but I did not let the fear rule me. I was just aware of its presence. After completing my tasks at hand, I realized that going out of my comfort zone was really healthy for me to have done. It showed me that I was capable of doing things that I didn't think I could do and once my tasks were completed, I tapped into inner strength that I didn't even know I had. I'm grateful that I went outside of my little box. I'm stronger for having done so!

What's the nicest thing (or things) that anyone has ever done for you? My life is so blessed, that it's difficult for me to single out just one thing, but if I had to, it would be a friend buying me a prosthesis after my first mastectomy (insurance didn't cover it at the time). He just gave me the money for it. Amazing act of kindness and an amazing feeling of gratitude from me.

I always thought that I was spiritually evolved enough to handle pretty much everything that life threw at me. Until my mother died. I broke. I really broke. As broken as a human being can be, I was. Watching her die over the last six months of her life was definitely life-altering for me. I lost my desire to live, because the one who had given me life ceased to exist. I wanted to be with my mother. After all, we had been together my entire life. In a way, her death prepared me for almost anything life could throw at me from that time on.

I always find that living in gratitude solves a multitude of prospective challenges. When I'm focused on gratitude, I cannot feel anything but happy and grateful. When I let that focus slip . . . well that's when the "stinkin' thinkin'" rears its ugly head! Being grateful is definitely the best tool to

use daily in order to live a loving and gracious life .
. .

Recently the topic of "triggers" has come up on several occasions with very different people. It becomes challenging for us when we are faced with something that triggers memories and/or behavior from the past. Awareness of the situation is the key, followed by action to change oneself. What are some of your triggers? How do you handle your triggers?

The soul is to our physical being as the sun is to the earth.

Imagination is incredible. You can be anywhere or do anything. You can achieve unrealistic feats of grandiosity. You can jump from galaxy to galaxy while cradling the earth in your arms .The trick is to use that imagination to help you stay in reality .How? By realizing that everything is temporary (as in one's imagination) and to keep on moving forward. Imagination is like hope in a way, it can't be taken away from you. In adversity, imagination and fantasy can be used as a tool to get you through your challenges.

Struggle. Why is making a decision or a choice so difficult sometimes? Why do we have such an inner struggle? Well, what I do is I let my imagination take me several years down the road and I look at how I would be feeling at that time about the outcomes of either decision I would have made, and see how it feels. Sort of trying it on. My present decision is based upon if I wished I had done it or if I would be glad that I didn't. I go with that feeling -- the projection of how I will be feeling in several years from now. For me, that seems to diffuse the struggle part in the present and allows me to easily decide upon which path I should pursue.

Do more of what makes you happy and live every moment of life to the fullest!!!! Grab opportunities when they are in front of you, as they may not be there if you wait!!!

What we think we see in others may not always be accurate. All of us change and evolve -- parts of our personality that were there many years back, may no longer be a part of us, we have grown, softened or hardened. We have become more or less emotional or caring. In short, we've changed. Others may not necessarily see that we've changed, and are basing their opinions of us on past experience and knowledge. Let's all look at what's before us now and let go of pre-conceived notions of others. Let's all make a true attempt to be more loving and accepting of others, setting aside pre-conceived notions.

Most people change, or evolve, during their lives. We certainly change physically! Yet, there are those who remain stagnant -- emotionally and spiritually. It is for those people who are so stagnant, just plugging through their every-day lives, that we must send some loving prayers. There are those who just don't get it, and perhaps never will. Let's all make an effort today to send loving vibes to others, OK?

Some people are still looking outside of themselves for inner strength, happiness, contentment, and they constantly say "I know" to absolutely everything. "I know" can be quite a barrier. Once we realize how little we actually "know," we open ourselves up to learning and growing within. When we open ourselves to inner growth, we have the ability to live in love and gratitude from within.

Looking within to see how you can grow or change is always the best way to handle the challenges throughout life. If you're feeling something other than love & gratitude, look within to see exactly what it is that you're feeling and attempt to understand what's going on inside of you to cause a blockage of energy.

When your family of origin chooses not to have you in your life, you begin to develop a family of choice. These become the people upon whom you can depend and love. It can be difficult when one's blood-related family chooses to divorce you. But remember, you have choices. You develop a new family of those who are loving and supportive. Think of the valuable life lessons from your situation.

Life is to be cherished – our friends often become our family, and they are to be cherished. Your new sisters, brothers, aunts, uncles, parents -- have heightened your awareness of life and because of that, you are evolving on your soul's journey, ever aware of the frailties of the earthly plane.

The perceptions of people that we hold on to may no longer be accurate. Once we look within ourselves and realize how we've changed, it becomes possible to realize that others may have changed as well, even though the outer shells look the same.

There's something to be said about looking at life through rose colored glasses. One of my favorite things in counseling people is to provide clients with a different viewpoint on their life's situation. I love hearing someone say "I never thought of it that way" while in the midst of chaos. Sometimes all that is needed to diffuse a situation is a pair of rose colored glasses to provide a new slant on life!!!

Enlightenment can present itself in many forms. Sometimes our enlightenment can be in the form of someone else's attitude or actions, often time showing us what we don't want to do or be like. Enlightenment can come in many forms.

Stains are to fabric as scars are to the body, as emotional pain is to the soul. Some stains come out, some remain.

Living & thinking outside of the box has brought me to a wonderful place of self-love & self-acceptance. Yes, I've worked hard to be where I am now. I have accomplished more than I could ever have imagined. I continue to learn, grow, be an individual, create, and love . . . how beautiful is it to live a life free from fear, shame, guilt? It's amazingly beautiful. I am truly blessed.

Interesting how some can throw everyone into the same category. Many think that their way of thinking, living, believing, is the only way of doing so. As much as we think we're accepting of others' ways, we most often want them to think how we think, act how we believe it's appropriate to act, believe the same things we believe. Everyone is different. There is not just one way of thinking, being or doing. What is "right" for one, may not be "right" for another. Just something to think about.

Some seek attention by living in their illness or disability; some seek attention by acting out their darkest fantasies; others seek attention by being different. Many like to live in their problems without seeking their solutions; they say that they want help to get or to be better, but are unwilling to follow through with whatever it would take to have them living in the solution -- it is their comfort zone, it is what they've known. Those who are accepting of where they are in their lives do not necessarily seek or need attention, but freely give to others quietly, with grace, dignity, and unconditional love.

I had the opportunity to speak with another breast cancer survivor last night who had been fired from her job. It brought back to mind that, during my trial, my former employer had stated that I had lost my skills (typing, shorthand, whatever else!) when I had my mastectomy. Yup. You heard it right. Today, when I read that part of of the trial over in my mind, I feel really, really grateful to be me. I created new law in New York State as a result of my trial. Gotta be grateful for all we go through in life . . . we're always in a position to help others, even though at the time, it appears that life gives us monstrous speed bumps . . .

When you have a true sense of yourself without the need of being something else, you project that into your life – into everything you do. Your vibrations change. Just be yourself, whatever that may be. You will quickly weed out those who are not your friends and equally as fast, you will have new friends in your life who have that same sense of self.

We are all given the opportunity to change from within. When we find ourselves in the same situation feeling the same way, multiple times – it's just the Universe testing us to see if we're going to handle things any differently, to see if we're evolving. When we begin to act and react in a new way, we have new situations facing us rather than the same ones repeatedly.   A lesson has been learned. We always have the opportunity to grow.

It's interesting how we can give people and/or situations such power over us – such control over us to make us feel angry, frustrated, emotionally drained. When we just listen to what's going on around us rather than absorbing the energy, we no longer give our power away. Nothing has the power to affect us, only the energy that we allow. I allow only positive, loving energy to enter into my realm. That's a great way to begin any day !!!

I'm not sure that I understand why anyone thinks they're less than perfect. We are all perfect beings in the loving eyes of the Universe. Is there any tree that is a less than perfect tree? I think not – every tree is a perfect creation. Aren't we all a perfect creation? Yes, we are all perfect beings. Move forward in your life as if you are that perfect being, bring love and blessings to everything you do and to everyone you encounter. See how your life can change because of an energy shift in your attitude !!! You are a perfect being.

When we take proper care of our physical body, our spiritual body and emotional body automatically fall into place -- we become balanced, physically, mentally and emotionally.

Why is it we give others such power over us? If we change our attitude to a more loving, accepting attitude, what anyone else says or does, or how anyone else acts, we don't give them power over us, and in so doing, we no longer harbor anger which turns into a resentment, which cripples us. We have the power to acknowledge what energy we allow into our being. Use that power!!!

It's rare that we can fully understand what someone else's life is like – sure, we can get the basics – it's hectic, tiring, etc. – but we can't necessarily comprehend the full emotional impact of anyone else's life. Methinks we need more compassion towards others.

Every day is filled with life and discovery. Every day is brand new and filled with its own miracles. I feel kind of sorry for those who think they're stuck in a routine -- all it takes is a change of attitude from within. Stay excited to see what's around the next corner!

When we allow stress into our lives, it changes our demeanor. I'm not saying that I never feel stressed out, but when I do allow stress to seep in, it's only temporary. Sometimes that stress can be motivating, as if I'm running on sheer adrenaline – which is fine – that works !! I realize that the stress I'm feeling is only temporary and that I've survived through many more of life's hurdles in the past. Whatever I perceive that I'm going through now is only a hiccup in life. It will soon pass and I will be a better person for having worked through it.

Questions. I've had many people ask me questions to which they really did not want an answer. Don't ask a question unless you are prepared to receive the answer.

Birth and Death are two sides of the same coin. One second you're not here and the next you are here (birth). One second you're here and the next you're not here (death).

Is there such a thing as "false" hope? Or is hope just hope, like love is just love? What one perceives as "false," another perceives as real, and it is true for them.

My truth is in my heart. Your truth is in your heart. They are different. I have learned to follow my path and to be true to myself. Our paths in life are different. It isn't necessarily easy to follow your path and to be true to yourself.

I've noticed that by living in love and gratitude and having complete faith that the Universe continuously watches over me, has truly changed my life. I have no stress. I have no worries. I am able to truly live happy, joyous and free. If I feel a petty annoyance, I send love and blessings to the person or situation, pull back the reins, and put myself back into the space of love and gratitude. Works like a charm.

Living in love and gratitude and approaching EVERYTHING with that love and gratitude keeps all other emotions out of the equation.

Interesting how others can give you so much power. You can become the subject of their gossip -- they won't attend a function because you are going to be there or they won't invite you to their function for various petty reasons. They find you important enough to make the subject of many conversations, yet they claim you are not wanted in their life. Fascinating how people can talk about you so much and think that they don't want you in their lives . . .

As much as we are powerless over others, that is how much power we have over ourselves.

You are actually the reason others are able to move forward and progress in their life. Your conversations and motivating words with others have given them the ability to move forward when they felt that they were moving backward. We're always in the position to help others. It's up to them how they use our energy, whether it be

through fear, jealousy, admiration, gratitude, or
motivation . . . It's up to them.

Mother Nature is a wonderful teacher. She shows
us that our lives have cycles, just as nature has its
seasons. I do my best to remember life's cycles
when I'm in the midst of any inner conflict (and
ALL conflict is inner). It is just a cycle. It will pass.
Funny, how we don't have to think about such
things while in the midst of "good" stuff!!!

The Winter Goddess is once again upon us,
embracing us with her blanket of love to keep us
warm during the colder months. She will watch
over us and provide what we need during the
winter. When we are blessed with snow, she
teaches us to be in awe of the beauty of Mother
Nature, for even snow and ice possess their own
beauty.

Someone said to me today that they were in the
pursuit of happiness. I felt sorry for that person.
Happiness is an inside job and they were in the
pursuit of happiness outside of themselves.

We should never have to struggle that hard with
our feelings or emotions. It is important to look
deep within to see where your struggle lies, then
make a shift in consciousness (or attitude) to
resolve your inner conflict.

Laughter is the sunlight of my soul. Gratitude is
my soul's reflection. Love is what I'm made of.

Embrace that which is causing you inner conflict and ask that the Universe show you your path to resolution.

When we have a problem with something -- whatever it may be -- we need to get to the root of it and arrive at a solution so that the problem does not take our energy. Problem = Blockage. When we have a blockage, we are stuck -- just like a dam blocks water -- it holds the water back so that it cannot flow -- a blockage (or problem) holds our energy back so that it cannot flow. We must find their origin so that we can remove our blockages. I'm not saying it's easy. Do you know where your problems come from?

If we have to think about controlling or managing anything in our lives (such as anger, overeating, drinking alcohol) we probably have to look much deeper into ourselves for solutions.

There is a certain flow of energy . . . when it works, you know it's flowing effortlessly and it feels really good. When the energy flow is blocked, you KNOW it effortlessly and it feels really good to change the direction of the energy flow. It may take a few tries to get it flowing in the right direction, but once you're aware that changes must be made, you have the ability to go with the flow!!!

A kind word, a smile on our face, opening the door for someone -- Think of some small way that you can brighten someone else's day today, then take action and do it! Getting out of ourselves and focusing on others helps us in many ways . . .

There are many different kinds of apples. Each has a distinct flavor, texture, color. Even within the same type of apple, you never find two exactly alike. They are all perfect in their own right. Just as we are perfect.

I find it so fascinating that when we begin to let go of things in the past, it frees us to enjoy our future. Our past can only have as much power over us as we permit it to have. I give it no permission.

I knew someone who went to work to a job they hated. In the morning while looking in the mirror, they would repeat many times over "I don't give a damn about anything." Just a little tool in letting go. I used to do that as well, and I found that it worked.   Kind of what they say today – "whatever." Just a tool to use to let go of things.

We may not always be aware of how our actions affect others. If you say you're going to call someone, then pick up the phone and call them. If you say that someone is your friend, you need to act like a friend. It all begins with awareness . . . how would you like to be treated by someone? Treat them accordingly. At least you will be doing your part . . .

Be aware of how you say things to others and remember that we each have our own priorities in life. My priorities are not yours and vice versa. I am respectful of what you do in your life and I expect to be treated with that same respect. That is a reasonable expectation.

Reasonable expectations. If you don't make an expectation, you cannot be disappointed. But there are times that expectations can be reasonable, such as expecting your car to start when you turn the key. That is reasonable. I also expect to be treated with kindness and respect by others, and I feel that is also reasonable. In the rare instances when I am treated rudely by another, I pray for that person, not knowing what is causing their lack of harmony in their life, but knowing that they need love and prayers more than I could imagine.

Sometimes it's necessary to just let go of things without analyzing or understanding. Just acknowledge its existence, and let it go.

We're all on a learning curve. Every one of us, every day. Try to remember that.

Live every moment in life as a new moment -- it really is new anyhow, even if we think we've done things before, we've not lived in this very moment before. Never make assumptions. Live with compassion and love for others.

Putting conditions on something rather than accepting unconditionally can bring disappointments and block our energy flow. Loving & Accepting unconditionally allows energy to flow and inspires us to grow rather than to stay stuck.

We may have a pre-conceived notion of what someone's personality is like from an impression left upon us from childhood or young adulthood.

As we mature, that impression may or may not change. The key is, to be aware that our earlier perception may not be accurate and that it needs to be revised. Many immature perceptions are based upon limited experience in life, yet we hold onto those perceptions throughout our life. Awareness is the key. Once we become aware that a person may be totally different than originally perceived, we can become open to embrace their inner beauty.

Many struggle with being true to themselves. It is more important to some to be accepted and a part of something rather than recognizing their own inner truths.

We must always be aware that toxic people do pop up in our lives. I choose to send them on their way with love and blessings, but not to have them participate in my life.

Living in fear is living without love. If you live in love and gratitude, there is no fear.

Some people think they know what their path in life is but are waiting for the right moment to take it. Others don't have to think about it, they just follow their path.

There was recently something going around FB about the glass being half empty/half full. The glass is always full. It's just that it's filled partially with water and the rest, with air. So . . . with regard to an empty box or an empty anything -- it's never empty. It is always full -- perhaps with air, but it is full. The lesson -- it's all a matter of perception.

I recently had the opportunity to interact with someone who was the anti-me – very little sociability, no grace, not a stitch of diplomacy, unenthusiastic and downright rude. This person was cold and lacked tact. It was interesting to me that I was able to observe this other person and realize that I really do have all of these qualities that people tell me I have !!! I am grateful that my path crossed with this person. I learned from our encounter. What a blessing others can be in our lives.

I noticed the other day that someone said something that I overheard, mind you, it wasn't even said to me, that pushed a button inside of me. I was aware enough to look within to see the origin of that "on" button, and was able to dismiss my emotions. I acknowledged them, but was able to move forward, and hopefully, grow enough so that if that same "on" button is toyed with at another time, it will have less impact and I'll be able to move on to the next challenge !!!

I've written often about triggers and about childhood hurts that we've carried into adulthood, as well as our insecurities that have followed along with us. But what about how we were and are perceived by others? I've heard people say that they don't like so and so from high school – or even grade school -- because he/she did this or that. They don't even know the person now, but they don't like them because of something that happened years and years ago. It could be something so trite as "they bumped into me in the playground and hurt my shoulder" all the while the person who bumped into the other person didn't even know they did it and has never understood why they haven't been liked or accepted. Something to think about as to how this would apply in your life.

Someone who was bullied or made fun of as a child may suffer from low self-esteem as an adult. Parents & siblings often can say or do things that make us feel not so good. And as a result, we may have various triggers, some triggers could be words; others, how someone else acted. Regardless, inner buttons get pushed. At some point, we need to become aware of our "buttons" so that we can work through our triggers. Once you can let go of your fears and insecurities, you are able to in love & acceptance rather than judgment and fear.

The only thing over which we have control is our own attitude. Remember that the next time you want to change someone else.

The first step towards inner change is awareness. Once we become aware, we are able to take action, and by taking action, we are able to grow.

How is a hope different from an expectation?

Love is absolute. It is not subject to interpretation. Love IS.

Taking responsibility for ourselves is a lesson to be learned in life. We tend to blame circumstances and people in the outside world over which we have no control for various situations and even our emotional state, playing a victim to life's varying situations. Once we take hold of the reins of our life and look within to change things in our life, the magic of life begins to unfold.

Forgiveness or accepting is not the condoning of another's actions, it is a gift you give yourself. The gift of freedom that comes along with accepting others, gives you the ability to move forward and realize that if another person wants to behave a certain way or do certain things, it is their choice and it has nothing to do with the awesome person you are!

You will feel so much better about absolutely everything in life when you learn to love unconditionally and be accepting of others. It is very freeing. When you harbor resentments, anger, fear, etc., you are blocked and will remain blocked until you learn to live in a place within yourself where there is just pure love.

I choose to not fight or argue with people, but rather to accept what they say -- I have no reason to be drawn into their anger. I just usually yes people to death, send them prayers, and walk away with a clear conscience, being my happy self.

What goes around comes around and no amount of whining, crying, revenge, or complaining will even come close to the beautiful justice of Karma. All that matters is that you are the best person you can be!

Do you choose to live in the problem or in the solution? Personally, I choose to live in the solution. We always have a choice. And usually that choice lies within our attitude.

Try approaching everyone you encounter with love, as if they've never experienced unconditional love before and you'd be the first to give it to them. And I mean everyone . . . if you find yourself having difficulty or friction with someone, make a conscious effort to pull yourself back and be aware of the direction of your thoughts. Change your thoughts to send that person love. Practice this on a regular basis. Remember, you can't play the piano or run track or do anything in life without repetition, which is practice.

You know how you only hear from certain people when they need something? Do you feel a little annoyed about that -- you know, that they only call you out of need? Well, let's look at that from a little bit of a different viewpoint . . . You're being called because they know that they can depend on you, you are reliable, steadfast and they need something from you, specifically, that only you can provide to them. It's really an honor to be of service and to help others . . . Try looking at it that way the next time someone calls you from out of the blue to ask a favor of you or needs something from you . . . Feel blessed, not angry. It's always nice that someone thinks of us and holds us in high regard, even though they may not even realize that's what they're doing !!!

Let others own their "stuff." It's our job to send them love & blessings.

We can only live in abundance when we're focused on the right thing: Living in Love & Gratitude.

Focus on the question rather than the answer. If you think about it -- a question is limitless whereas an answer is finite. Once you have an answer, a blockage occurs and it's finished -- can't go further. If you keep yourself open to questions, always questions, you are always open. How can I improve myself? Show me what more can be . . . Endless . . . Always keep the door open . . .

One of the most difficult things is to learn to let go, and to let others run or ruin their lives, especially when we sincerely care or love them.

If someone is trying to pick a fight or to argue with you, you have the power to diffuse the situation. How? Well, what I do is just say that I feel differently, or we will have to agree to disagree, or that's what makes horse races or something to not go into someone else's stuff. You have power and control your own attitude. No one can take that away from you unless you allow it to happen.

Everything we think we know is a direct result of how we perceive it to be based upon our experiences in life. Love is not subject to perception.

If we look for the "whys" in life, we may be distracted in living our lives to the fullest. Rather than asking "why," just be grateful for whatever it is about which you're asking "why," accept it, and move on.

Many people are living their lives in the absence of love and compassion towards others. All it takes is a slight shift in attitude to heighten awareness and become more loving and compassionate . . .

It is our past behavior that has brought us to our present behavior, both through our actions and our words. We are the sum of all of the parts of our life.

Failure is a matter of skewed perception. A shift in attitude and you see a perceived "failure" as part of your pathway to success . . .

 Let's all try to remember that the written word carries no emotions -- others cannot necessarily see that we're joking with them or that we're trying to be witty or silly -- the written word subjects itself to misinterpretation and misunderstanding. Just something to keep in mind.

Today I am so grateful to be me -- Living in love and gratitude allows me such emotional freedom.

We have to be grateful for even the things in our lives that we perceive to be so horrific, they're unfathomable, but they're a part of us and we're better people because of all of our experiences in life.

When we let go of old beliefs and emotions, the Universe bestows upon us the true meaning of life and how beautiful it is, allowing us to live openly in love and gratitude.

Man & man's ego have created much of the "rules" by which we live. For me, my rules are in my soul and I have learned to be true to myself, not to be true to what is right for someone else. I simply live in love and gratitude, and the rest of my life falls miraculously into place!

Keeping an open mind can be challenging at times, as most of us tend to hold onto old belief systems and keep our stubborn opinions and thoughts well in tact! Being aware is the first step to keeping an open mind. If we look at everything and everyone as presenting us with something new all the time, it becomes easier to be receptive to new ideas, thoughts, and behavior. Today, I will listen, just listen, to what others have to say, as I never know where I will be learning something new.

It's amazing to me how wealthy I've become since I stopped measuring my wealth with money.
When we live in love and gratitude, our inner wealth abounds! The rest follows suit . . .
Amazing . . . Blessings all . . .

When you eliminate something (or someone) from your life, you open the door for something (or someone) new to replace it . . .

The fairy of spring has waived her magic wand over the seeds the winter goddess has left behind -- soon to be blooming flowers, trees, vegetables - - how beautiful!!!

There are always two sides to every story.
Trouble is, that most people choose to judge upon
only hearing one side rather than knowing the
whole story.

In order to have success in life we must pay our
dues, in doing some things that may not seem so
successful. Remember, that everything we do is a
stepping stone to our ultimate success . . . All
experiences, all changes within, everything --
they're all stepping stones.

Every moment I live from this point on is a bonus.
Every person that crosses my path in life from this
point on is a bonus. Everything that I experience
from this point on is a bonus. That is how I see
my life.

What does faith mean to you? To me, it means
that I know something other than tangible is on my
side. Faith is a feeling that there is a force greater
than I watching over me. Faith is not religious and
does not have religious connotations. Faith is
knowing, in your heart of hearts, that there is a
power or a force or an energy greater than I am
that is with me. Some may choose to call that
power God, some may call it Jesus, some may call
it Buddha, some may call it The Universe -- it
doesn't much matter what you call it -- it's still the
same thing -- faith . . .

One thing that two bouts with cancer has taught
me -- don't sweat the small stuff. No, wait -- don't
sweat anything -- the Universe has a far greater
plan than I could ever imagine -- I have absolutely

no control of anything except my own attitude, and I choose to live in love and gratitude. That's what I've learned.

Always remember that what someone thinks, feels and says about you has nothing to do with you and everything to do with them.

Respect. Self-respect is honoring and loving you. Respect for others is honoring and loving them. When you honor self-respect, you honor your commitments by keeping your word, showing up on time for appointments because you are honoring your self-worth, your good intentions. When you respect others, you honor your commitments by keeping your word, showing up on time for appointments – you are showing that you honor others. What does respect mean to you?

You will have many deep-seeded learning experiences for your life. The lessons will not be learned all at once, but gradually, your inner being will grow and you will be able to move forward with beautiful love and light . . . Live in love and gratitude as much as you can. Live in unconditional acceptance of others (all others, including your family) as much as you can. Let the burden you carry so heavily on your shoulders be lifted by living in love and gratitude, and by having faith that there is an invisible source watching over you and guiding you always.

I find it amazing that people that you've known during your life turn out to be different from how you perceived them to be initially. My mother gave me fair warning, but I chose not to listen, thinking that they couldn't be all that bad, now – could they? I'm not sorry that I didn't heed her words of wisdom, as I had to draw my own conclusions and learn my own lessons in my own time.

When I look at the ocean, I don't necessarily think of the life that is underneath the water and I certainly don't see the life that is underneath the water. Aren't people like the ocean? Don't we look at one another without knowing what's going on underneath the surface of what we see? Maybe we all need to heighten our awareness and compassion towards each other and realize that there is always more to something or someone than what we are seeing.

If I disagree with someone's actions or words, I take a step back to realize that I am not in their shoes. How they are is right for them at that moment.

Often, I find that situations throughout the day make me very grateful that I'm me.

We are all moving along swimmingly in this beautiful ocean of life . . . . Some of us can swim better than others. Some use different strokes. Some are underwater, while others sail on top of the water. However you move in the ocean of life is the right movement for you.

Only thoughts of beautiful things -- butterflies, rainbows, smiles, love -- are allowed to live rent-free in the apartments of my mind. All other thoughts must find dwelling elsewhere . . .

Even though I am very trusting of others, when their disrespect shows me that I have used poor judgment, I will not permit cynicism to prevail. I will still look at others with love and trust until they show me otherwise, at which point, I will let them go from my life with love and blessings.

The term "Christ Consciousness" really has nothing to do with believing in Christ or being a Christian. I neither believe in Jesus in the traditional sense, nor am I a Christian. But . . . the term "Christ Consciousness" refers to a higher sense of being, of being a being of love and light and living in love, gratitude and being kind, loving and accepting of others. It has taken me some time to learn this and to let go of "old" religion.

Observing others becoming angry and/or impatient and/or upset about things in life has become interesting to me. Living in love & gratitude, it is rare that I experience these negative emotions, and if they creep into my life, they are fleeting. I am very grateful that I live in a peaceful place of love & gratitude.

We've all been given the gift of life -- what's amazing to me is how everyone uses that gift so differently!

Everything in life is a lesson. Others continue to teach me well. I continue to pray that I may be mindful, respectful and loving toward others.

If you feel tension or annoyance with someone or something, look within . . . as the answer to your discomfort is usually something inside of yourself that needs a little tweaking . . .

Everything in life is a lesson. Others continue to teach me well. I continue to pray that I may be mindful, respectful and loving toward others.

Each of us is on a different journey with ultimately the same destination.

If you witnessed someone's behavior or actions several years ago and you're basing your opinion of them upon that past behavior, perhaps it's time to get to know that person. What they did or how they acted in the past doesn't mean that they're that same person today as they were in the past. Let's do our best to be aware of old opinions and judgments, and re-think our emotions.

 Our paths in this lifetime are what heighten our spirituality and our capacity for love.

Often when we have trouble with something, or feel conflict or discomfort, such as a title that someone has or a descriptive word, it has to do with an experience we've had in the past. Possibly with a person of a certain title or the way we were treated by someone we were supposed to have trusted, or what someone said to us. We have to dig deep into our memory to understand why we feel this way and it may not be pleasant. But once we work through our feelings, we are a better and stronger person. Is there is a deep seeded insecurity or lack of self-esteem? Do you

feel inferior? Do you have low self-confidence?
Exactly what is it that is bothering you about
someone or something? What exactly makes you
feel the emotion you're experiencing? Who said
something or what happened to you that is
causing your discomfort?

When we talk (or even THINK) about someone or
something, we are giving that someone or
something energy.

Being around other people's disfunctionality is a
gentle reminder from the universe that I must
continuously send love and blessings to those less
fortunate than I. I must always send love &
blessings to others.

When you cease to make expectations, you will
not have disappointments. When you begin living
in love and gratitude, your life will have a beautiful
flow and energy to it all the time.

My thoughts are the seeds of life implanted in my
mind. My actions are the flowering results . . .

We have absolutely no control over others.
Accepting them with all of their flaws and
shortcomings is what we need to do in order to live
in a peaceful place within our own souls.

We are all teachers and we are all students.

In spite of everything, I still hope beyond hope,
believe beyond belief and even if people in my life
are dishonest, I know that The Universe has a far

more grand plan for me (and them!) and I keep my faith knowing that I am on the right path.

Most of the time we simply have to do the best that we can with what we have.

We don't always need to know the reason for things that happen in our lives as they're happening, but somewhere down the line, the reason (our lesson) becomes apparent.

Today I am giving 100% of me to my life and everyone in it.

When writing to someone or speaking to someone, choose your words carefully. Be aware of your intent ... your purpose. Does it serve any purpose whatsoever to say anything negative? Probably not. Speak how you would like to be perceived.

It is such an honor to do a favor for a friend.

To everyone with whom I have crossed paths so far in this life – Thank you. For everyone with whom I have yet to connect – Looking forward to it! I am blessed to have learned all the lessons that I have learned so far because our paths have crossed . . . Without you, I wouldn't be me.

What are the ingredients for your recipe of a perfect day?

Today, I embrace all the beautiful colors of my world -- even the shades of gray -- ALL the colors .
. .

Why? I don't know. I don't know any "why's." I just have faith that The Universe is guiding me. If I ever need to know "why" about anything, I have to look within.

Fear of the unknown or excitement of what is yet to be. It's your choice.

I always have to remind myself to look within when something is bothering me.

Every experience we have in life is a learning experience -- provided life is approached with an open mind!

We may not always know why the Universe is guiding us in a certain direction, but at one point or another, it will become evident. Just have faith.

I was observing a buzzard flying the other day. It was soaring in very large clockwise circles and moving with the wind currents. There were low clouds, and he was cruising through some of the clouds and looked so relaxed and like he was in tune with his universe. I thought how wonderful that was and that we should all be soaring so effortlessly in our own lives. The Universe watches over us and guides us -- we just have to show up . . . Pretty cool.

How does one cope with challenging emotions? I do my best to acknowledge what I'm feeling. I honor my feelings, as they are real, but not necessarily wanted, I allow myself to feel whatever it is that I'm feeling (if it's not a fun emotion), and then I make a decision to let those negative emotions go and let the Universe take care of them.

We've all felt rejection at one time or another. Somehow, it never feels good. How does one feel rejected? Usually, there is an expectation involved and someone said something or acted in a way other than what we had expected. So, it seems that to avoid rejection, we need to be more accepting of others. In becoming more accepting of others, we release the expectations that can cause a rejection.

Stop focusing on what you think you don't have and just live in the gratitude for what you DO have! Live in the gratitude . . .

It is such a blessing that our paths cross and we intersect with such a variety of people and situations during our time on the physical plane.

Sometimes, it's not so much that people are "siding" with anything, so much that they just don't know how to be different than how they were brought up. Not everyone has a heightened sense of awareness to be open enough to live in a place from within of unconditional love. It takes awareness to change our old belief systems.

I have recently found myself disheartened by people by whom I was treated with a lack of respect. Though my heart is sad, I continue to send loving prayers to others who have yet to find their way.

What the heck is a "problem" anyhow? A problem is a temporary challenge that will be resolved.

If someone is judging you based upon their past and they're not willing to re-think their judgments, we need to send them loving prayers in hopes that they will be able to let go of their fears that bind them so. It is when we're blocked with pre-conceived notions that we are unable to move forward.

Perception is interesting. There are those who react with ego. There are those who act out of acceptance. There are those who consistently look outside of themselves and "blame" others. There are those to know that when something feels uncomfortable to look within. Perception.

Living in love and gratitude means living in peace within. You just somehow KNOW that the Universe will provide and things are going to be OK.

Sometimes, no matter how carefully I am to choose my words, there is still mis-perception. Being that I live in love and gratitude, my intent is never to be mean or sharp-tongued in any fashion. Yet, people still live in a place other than where I live within myself, and still mis-perceive, and still hear their interpretation of what they want to hear, not what was actually said. Amazing.

If you spend your life trying, all you can do is try. If you spend your life planning, all you will do is plan. It is only upon taking action that you can DO!!

I find it interesting that many still attempt to think outside their box, still thinking that there's a box.

I'm rather happy that I can be naïve sometimes. It keeps me focused on most of the good things in life without realizing the potential icky-ness of any situation. A blessing in disguise I suppose.

I am happy -- inside and out -- it's taken me a lot of inner work to get there, but I have arrived, and absolutely no one has my permission to make me angry, unkind, unloving, or anything else that they want me to be or feel.

You know how excited you feel when you embark on a vacation? You get all of these great feelings rushing through you. Well, that's the way life should be on a daily basis. Life is a journey -- filled with trials and tribulations -- much like the perfect vacation, complete with a perfect beach or a mountain stream; a rude flight attendant and your lost luggage arriving a day late (minor annoyances). Focus on the good things. In the long run, enjoy this magnificent journey of life with all its twists and turns!

Today, I'm excited about my life's journey. I'm looking forward to new adventures and moving forward.

You know how sometimes you really want something so badly you can taste it and then the Universe comes along and gives you something entirely different, which ultimately becomes better than what you had originally wanted? Remember that the next time you want something really badly and the Universe brings you something entirely different!

The fantasies about any given situation are most often far more grandiose in our minds than reality. Unless, of course, you're at the Oscars and you're on stage making your acceptance speech. That reality might just be better than the fantasy.

I have the control to do something about my situation . . . many times, it's as simple as re-adjusting my attitude; other times, maybe it's cleaning out my life, whether it be of people or "stuff." Either way, I have the choice . . . I have the power . . . I have the control of me . . .

We've all heard that it's the journey, not the destination, that counts. Nothing could be more true of life itself . . . Enjoy the journey of your life!

Commitment. Making a commitment to do one thing doesn't prevent you from doing other things. It simply means that ultimately, you carry out what it is you said you would do, and stick to it. Giving our word and keeping our word are important to our inner growth.

I am grateful for the fact that I'm able to love unconditionally and that the Universe has taught me acceptance. Living in love and gratitude is amazing. I have incredible people in my life and I am so blessed.

It's great to have goals. We all have them. It's important to remember to set goals that are attainable -- start off with small goals that you know you can accomplish. Even a shopping list is a goal !!! When we have a "to do" list and we cross off what we've done, one by one -- we're achieving goals. By accomplishing attainable goals, we set the stage so that we can strive toward goals that may be somewhat more complex.

Trust & Love. Petunia's taught me something very important about love and trust. She trusts me unconditionally and with that trust, comes unconditional love. I don't know how I've earned that trust from her and because she's my pet, she can't really tell me in human words. But I do know that there is unconditional love and trust that is mutual. Why is there a challenge in human to human relationships for unconditional love & trust?

Setting healthy boundaries is great. Keep in mind that not all boundaries are healthy. If a boundary is created out of fear or dissention, it is not coming from the right place. A healthy boundary must come from self-respect and self-love.

It's so difficult when we make expectations -- and we ALL make expectations -- and we're disappointed because of those expectations. The more we live in acceptance and unconditional love, the less we project into the future and create potential disappointments. Not easy, but it can be done!!

It's very easy to be critical or judgmental of others who walk a different path than we do. Sometimes it's helpful to picture yourself in someone else's shoes and see how you would like to be treated.

When you start doing things because they're the right things to do and not for recognition, praise or ego inflation, you are on a spiritual path.

I am so blessed that I am comfortable enough within my own skin to be happy and totally free and 100% me!!!

It's interesting when our emotions are triggered. Like when something you thought you were completely over on an emotional level is brought back to life, evoked by something that was said, causing you to feel things you didn't know you still had inside of you to feel.

There is a difference in being grateful and living your life in love and gratitude. When you live your life in love and gratitude, there is no room for unhappiness or depression.

Often, I will begin to write something and then I sit back to look at my words. Am I keeping everything positive? I want to make sure than my words are conveying the right intention. I often ask what purpose will these words serve, before I say them or write them. If nothing positive can come of my words, I either re-phrase what I was going to say or keep my mouth shut. Choose your words carefully.

Looking outside this morning, I felt an overwhelming sense of gratitude -- the beautiful blue sky, the trees losing their summer green hues, the air so crisp and clean. What are you grateful for today?

It's so easy to remember the "good" stuff in life that has brought us happiness. But isn't it equally as important to remember the "bad" stuff that has brought us challenges in the form of valuable lessons? Personally, I don't think anything is really good or bad, it just is; and as for lessons, there is a lesson in pretty much everything whether we perceive it to be good or not so good.

When push comes to shove, there are very few people willing to do whatever it takes in order to change something with which they're unhappy. Unhappiness or discomfort can be somewhat of a comfort zone for some, and most people do not want to move past their comfort zone.

Instead of letting fear get the best of you, when you feel that emotion (fear) make a conscious decision to change it to excitement. Be excited about the circumstances or situation rather than fearful. It is a choice.

The next time you feel that you don't have time to do this or that, take a second and really think about it. The ONLY time you have is right now -- life is precious and way too short -- do things that bring you (and/or others) joy and happiness. This is all we've got here folks !

Why question your divinely driven intuition? Problems occur when we think too much with our "logical" minds rather than moving along with our intuitive "minds." If you follow your inner voice, or intuition, which is divinely driven, what questions or doubts could one possibly have? Trust your inner voice.

Achieving a goal can be somewhat challenging on occasion. When we feel stuck, we tend to procrastinate. Instead of letting your goal overwhelm you, make your progress towards it in baby steps. Break your goal down into steps moving in the direction of achieving the ultimate goal. In essence, you are connecting the dots to the goal a little bit at a time -- keep it simple !!

I am grateful that I'm able to realize that when I feel discomfort within, it's not usually the fault of anyone outside of me, though something what was said or done has triggered my feelings. It's up to me to look inside of myself and discover what's caused my discomfort so that I can take appropriate steps to heal my inner wounds.

I feel a little bit sad for those who are so opinionated that they are unable to look within.

When fear or anxiety rears its ugly head in your life, pull back the reins, be in the moment an start saying thank you to The Universe for all that you have !!!

Often, when I choose a parking spot, I will choose a parking spot that is the farthest away from where I'm going. It feels good to walk that extra distance. It gives me a little more exercise than I would normally get. Walking helps to clear my mind. The point that I'm getting to is that sometimes the shorter, easier route (to anywhere) is not always the best. Taking one's time and enjoying the journey is what it's all about.

Things happen to us or around us to help us to put things into perspective.

Interesting how life sends us little angels just at the time when we need them most.

We all face various challenges throughout our lives. We have the choice to choose our attitude towards those challenges. I choose to be grateful, loving and accepting. If I fall from my values of being grateful, loving and accepting, a blockage appears. At that time, I take a step back and examine what's going on inside of me. Why do I feel anything other than gratitude? What deep-seeded emotions are being triggered? When I get to the bottom of it all, I am then able to return to being myself and living in the moment. I'm not saying that it's always easy, but then again, it's all part of the journey.

I like to take moments throughout the day to focus on one thing -- can even be picture that someone posted on Facebook or one of my own photos -- to meditate and regroup.

We must always remember to do what's right for ourselves and to be true to ourselves when following our paths in life.

You gain knowledge from experience, but you don't gain experience from knowledge.

I always allow myself to feel whatever emotion(s) I'm feeling at any given time. I respect what I'm feeling or going through. I let it live within until it is ready to be lifted. When it is lifted, I am a much better person for having experienced my emotions.

Living in the solution and moving forward is just so much easier and lighter than wallowing in the problem and remaining stuck.

I am grateful that I am me and that I'm strong enough so that I don't feel it necessary to change for others and to be something other than me.

To the Universe: Thank you for putting all the people in my life with whom I cross paths. They are my teachers.

When we are blind-sided by someone's unkind actions or words, it is important to pull back the reins and focus. Send that person love and blessings, as they need it far more than could be imagined and be grateful for whatever experience you have encountered. All of our experiences in life help us to grow and become better people. Remember to live in the love and gratitude . . .

It is only the things that I HAVEN'T done in my life that I regret. Everything else, I'm grateful for having had those experiences as they have always enriched my life. I have minimal regrets for some things I haven't done -- at least not yet!!!!!

Opportunity. If we have an opportunity to do something or say something we should take it at

that very moment. A missed opportunity can lead
to a regret . . . whereas, if you take action on that
opportunity, there is no regret -- you are moving
forward instead of playing the shoulda, coulda
,woulda's . . .

When something occupies your mind and you go
back and forth on whether or not you should or
shouldn't do something, chances are you won't
feel at rest until you DO that something, cause if
you don't you will be telling yourself that you
should have done it !!! I've not yet regretted
anything I've done . . . only that which I haven't
done . . .

Do not mistake someone's kindness, love and
compassion for weakness.

When people gossip or talk about someone, they
are really giving power to the subject of their
conversation. In a sense, they're sending energy
to that person.

As much as all of the people that enter our lives
are teachers to us, we have to remember the other
side of the coin – that we are teachers to those
teaching us as well !!! Wild, huh?

Hope. Having hope can motivate you to keep
going.

Interesting how people think how others may
perceive them as weak or that they're being used
as a door mat. If we perceive ourselves as being
a door mat or being walked all over by others, at
any time, that is a reflection of low self-confidence

or low self-esteem. When we have higher self-esteem and self-confidence, the perception of others does not matter. We need to let others own their own "stuff." If someone has negative thoughts or perceptions, those are not our thoughts or perceptions.

Even if someone is nasty or rude to you, do not stoop to their level and return their rudeness or nastiness. Live your life being true to yourself and approach all situations with compassion, acceptance, love and kindness. That person who was unkind to you needs your loving vibrations more than you can possibly imagine. Live in love & gratitude. Accept others and don't allow yourself to act in a negative way because of how someone else acts or acted towards you.

What is it about being human that makes us so opinionated and judgmental towards others? I think we all need to realize that we never know a book by its cover. Just because someone looks a certain way to you doesn't mean they ARE a certain way. Be mindful.

Remember that there is no light without darkness. There is no darkness without light. To every action there is an equal and opposite reaction. If we didn't experience difficulties, we would not experience happiness.

It's fascinating to me how words that mean something really great to one person can have a negative connotation for someone else. I find the word "excitement" to be just that, enthusiastic, exciting and giving me something to look forward to. Someone else may not like the word "excitement," as it may provoke feelings of anxiety or bring up something to them from their past that is unpleasant. Choose your words carefully. Try to be more descriptive and remember that the person to whom you are writing or speaking does not know what's going on inside of your head.

Acceptance of others is not always easy. We tend to be judgmental and base our opinions upon how we're feeling and what we're going through at any given moment. We don't see that someone is grieving a loss of a loved one. We don't see that they're losing their home. We don't see that they've just lost their job. We don't see their health challenges. We do not see pain in another's soul. Next time you find yourself being judgmental towards someone, take a mental step back. Realize that you cannot physically see what's going on in someone else's life . . . inside of them. Have love, compassion and kindness toward others. Accept them with love at that moment – a loving thought/prayer or even a smile could change their life.

Before you speak, take a moment to be aware of the intent of your words and choose your words in accordance with your intent.

Interesting how some people have absolutely no sense of humor, harbor such anger within and are constantly looking outside of themselves to blame others

I need to be reminded to breathe. I know that sounds silly, but when I say to myself or someone else says "breathe," it pulls back the focus from life's craziness – it's almost a form of meditation . . . Try it – Breathe . . . Breathe . . . focus on your breath – don't you feel a little better? I know I do !!!

You have to take advantage of opportunities in life when they are presented to you. If you wait, those opportunities may be gone – never to appear again.

Water, Wind – can't see wind, yet it can create extensive damage as well as refreshing breezes. Water, liquid – fluid – refreshing to swim in, hydrates our bodies – can't live without it, yet it can create extensive damage. Mother Nature teaches us so much . . . . everything in moderation . . .

Remember the saying: "If you haven't got anything nice to say, don't say it at all"? Well, remember that saying and practice it!!

Many people do not understand that being true to oneself is not the same as the truth from within for each of us, and hence, they make judgments based upon the fact that someone's truth is different from theirs. I embrace your inner truth and accept it, even though it is different from my inner truth.

Part of life becomes un-fun when you thought you could trust someone and it turns out that you couldn't. That's always a tough lesson, one that most of us have experienced more than once !!!

When we learn our lessons in life, we become stronger having moved through them and coming out the other side of the tunnel so to speak. Not always an easy journey, but we're stronger and more experienced in life because of our experiences.

I feel grateful that the Universe guides me on my path . . . I am grateful for those whose with whom I cross paths during my journey . . . I give love, prayers & gratitude for all that I am and to everyone for all of the lessons I'm being taught and teaching to others . . .

Holding on to anger, resentment, or any other feeling or emotion that is not positive, serves absolutely no purpose. While holding on to these feelings, one becomes stagnant and unable to move forward. When we live in love and gratitude, accepting and embracing the negativity, we can begin to progress and move forward.

We have to remember to let others "own" their stuff. If someone makes an unkind remark, that remark belongs to them, not to you. If someone speaks unkind words about another, those words and emotions belong to them, not to you. We all have a choice as to whether or not we want to keep such people in our lives

Squirrels climb trees very well, without effort or thought. Their biggest thought is which tree they will climb. An elephant can't climb a tree. Does that mean that the elephant's a failure? No, the elephant is not a failure. The elephant is different from the squirrel. The squirrel is a perfect squirrel.

The elephant is a perfect elephant. How are any of us less than perfect beings in our own right?

Some people feel a sense of entitlement—as if they're owed something and they take advantage of what they perceive to be their privileges. I hope that I don't ever feel that sense of entitlement and that I am always aware of living in love and gratitude.

Use every day as it's meant to be -- a brand new day, a brand new beginning; think brand new thoughts . . . be positive . . . live in love and gratitude . . . send love to others even if you feel they've harmed you . . . Use this brand new beautiful day to your advantage !!!

There is a wonderful fluidity in one's life when living life from the core, or soul.

My attitude is everything – If I'm willing to change my attitude towards something, my perception of "that something" shifts. Works all the time in every situation.

All of us could probably use a little improvement on our listening skills. Rather than waiting to say something back, just be in the moment and listen, without the anticipation of speaking.

We've been brought up anticipating various events in our life -- to look forward to them, and along with that anticipation comes expectation -- the expectation we create in our minds that something is going to be a certain way, and when things don't pan out the way we expected, we are disappointed. We can avoid the disappointment associated with unrealistic expectations by living in the moment in love and gratitude. When we live in the moment, we can be grateful for whatever the outcome of a situation is without disappointment from an expectation.

Whatever we are giving thought to, we are giving energy to -- whether it be fear, joy, love, hate -- whatever it is. I give my energy to love and gratitude. I may not be able to control others, but I certainly can control me. So, I choose love and gratitude.

Everything in life is so fleeting and temporary. Life is very short. Let go of things that don't serve you in a positive way. Have the courage to change what you can. And know that the only thing you can ever control is your attitude towards anything.

When we're born, in the beginning we sleep a lot. Our lives consist of eating, eliminating and sleeping. Then we grow up and start learning all kinds of stuff and we live our lives. Then, in the blink of an eye, we're old and at the end of our lives -- back to eating, eliminating and sleeping.

Treating others with unconditional love and kindness is not necessarily an easy task to accomplish all the time. But, if we keep in mind how we would like to be treated by others and if we think before we act or speak, it becomes easier to treat others as we would like to be treated by them.

We all have a journey, and it always includes moving through and passing unpleasantries in order to get to the good stuff. And there's always good stuff.

I do not hold on to anger or resentments – they serve no constructive purpose. Living in love and gratitude allows me to instantly turn around any anger or resentment that may creep into my life.

Whatever we focus on is where we're giving our energy. If we focus on what we DON'T want, we're giving energy to that. If we focus on our fears, that's where our energy is going. Personally, I focus on what I DO want and my gratitude . . . and sending love and prayers to others.

Being less cynical is not always easy. Our lives are fast paced. Most of us are used to sarcasm. When I find myself being cynical, I pull back the reins and bring myself back into a place of gratitude, reminding myself that I want to live in place from within that is filled with unconditional love and kindness towards all.

Interesting sometimes how people who claim to be a friend are just never there for you when you need them, never able to talk when you need to, not there for you at all. Yeah, I know – we all have stuff going on in our lives, but it's also important to take a moment and understand that if someone needs us, we should be there for them – whether it's a long-term friend, or someone we've recently met.

Life has shown me that you do not always get what you give. I have experienced many un-evolved souls saying and/or doing things in my presence that is incongruent with me, who I am, and how I live my life. I keep these people in my thoughts and send loving prayers to them daily.

When someone expresses themselves in a negative fashion or without good intentions, that person is showing you what they're made of. When someone expresses themselves in a positive fashion with good intentions that person is showing you what they're made of. It's best to pay attention and to do our best to accept others with love and grace realizing that we're all in different stages of growth in our lives.

How wrongly we can come to judgments or assumptions about others based upon what we perceive them to be because of how they act or look, what they believe, or even where they live. Best to keep an open mind and lovingly accept others without judgment.

We are not responsible for someone else's words or actions. We are only responsible for our own words or actions.

Each person is born the same and dies the same. Sure, there are some minor differences which are for the most part external, but the essence is the same. What makes anyone think that the time between being born and dying is that much different for each of us? Again, there are some differences, but they are external. What we are made of -- our inner self -- is pretty much the same

for everyone. We are souls inside a physical shell
of a body. I'm not saying that everyone handles
what they're given in a like manner, but the
essence of what we are is the same for all. The
differences between us lie in what we do with
ourselves from the inside . . .
Our perceptions are often inaccurate. We may
perceive someone as being hostile, when in fact
it's our own hostility that we are seeing. What we
see in others is often a mirror of what is within us
at any given moment.

I always feel that we should take action and move
forward in life, but sometimes it's necessary to
pause and think about what that action is going to
be, except when spontaneity is in the air and an
instantaneous decision is required! It happens . . .

Remember to embrace others with unconditional
love and compassion today.

I was talking with a friend of mine not too long ago
and the subject of our pasts came up. She said to
me "Can you believe how screwed up we both
were?" I don't remember what my reaction was,
but I know that I was thinking HUH? To me, both
of us were in the appropriate emotional state at
that time for what we were going through. I think
that's the difference between being truly troubled
(or "screwed up") and well-adjusted -- when you're
"screwed up" you don't move past that point of
being screwed up and you don't grow and change
from your experiences, you hold on to what's
happened in your life and get stuck there. When
you're well-adjusted you pass through life's
challenges, let go of them and realize that they've

been amazing learning experiences that move you forward in your spiritual evolution.

I do my best to choose my words carefully so that they are accurately expressing my intent, but I've noticed that the written word is still subject to an interpretation other than my intent.

You may never know how much of a difference your actions or words have made in someone's life.

Fear, Anger and Anxiety are the absence of love and gratitude.

Interesting how when we were young we wanted to do things because someone else was doing them and we thought it was cool and would be "accepted" if we did it too. That doesn't necessarily change as we get older. It only changes as we have a secure sense of self from within. When we are secure within ourselves, then we can make our own decisions and not be concerned with what others do or what they may think.

If I see a piece of trash in my path I will make the effort to pick it up and throw it into the garbage pail -- wherever I am. Sometimes I catch myself looking at the litter and I begin to walk past it. I turn myself right around, pick up that piece of trash and throw it away. It may not seem like much, but doing something small like that on a regular basis is character building. When you discipline yourself to do something over and over again, you're creating a new habit. This can carry through on other areas of your life as well.

Happiness and Healing are both inside jobs. Next time you look outside of yourself for either one, remember to pull back the reins and to look within . . .

I found myself mentally reviewing my upcoming week and I began to feel totally overwhelmed. I kept saying to myself that I 'have' to do this and that. I realized that my words had much to do with how I was feeling. When I changed the word "have" to "want" the pressure lifted off of my shoulders. When I kept saying that I have to do something, it was creating anxiety and stress. In changing that one word, from "have" to "want" I shifted my energy.

I'm always one to smell the roses -- literally. The other day I was in the doctor's office, just after Valentine's Day, and there was a beautiful bouquet of peach roses on the counter. I went over to smell them, but they were the kind that didn't have a particularly rosey kind of smell to them. Maybe that was because they were artificial. Didn't stop me from smelling them!

Changing your attitude is something over which you have control. If you're feeling uncomfortable about something or angry, acknowledge that which is seemingly causing your inner discomfort and make a conscious decision to move on. What I do is thank The Universe for giving me this learning experience.

Being that our lives are based upon memory (think about it, early learning is about repetition/memory) focus on the good memories. The good memories are the ones you have to keep with you during challenging times. Remember that special sunset, that deep-down belly laughter, the best concert ever . . . remember the beautiful moments in your life and allow them to raise your vibrations.

What a blessing it is that "his-story" has been passed down for generations upon generations. Where would we be without history?

People have a tendency to condemn what they don't understand or know. Rather than being judgmental, how about finding out more about that which you have cultivated such strong feelings. The why's in life shouldn't matter too much . . . unconditional love and acceptance are what matter.

If you focus on what you don't want, you are giving energy to what you don't want and it will come to be. Try giving energy in a more positive light -- to what you DO want -- and you will achieve what you want ! Works like a charm . . .

Wonderful. Filled with wonder. I choose to be filled with wonder every day. Therefore, my life is wonderful. Everything that occurs in my life is filled with that same wonder because it is the first time that each moment in my life is happening. Every moment is filled with wonder. Wonderful.

It's OK that someone holds different beliefs from you. It doesn't make them or us bad people. We

are all different. We are all individuals. We share
some of our belief systems with others. Then
there are those with whom we do not share our
belief systems. Remember that we are all
different. Be kind and loving towards others, even
if they think differently from you.

One of our greatest challenges as humans is to
ride over life's speed bumps. Sometimes our
speed bumps in life seem insurmountable. But,
somehow, we make it to the other side wiser and
stronger than we were before.

Yes, it's true that your thoughts can become
reality. But that is not always the case. There are
many times when we think things, perhaps in
fantasy or "wishful" thinking, that we know are not
going to be reality. Then there are the thoughts
we have upon which we take action and our
thoughts become reality. Thoughts can go either
way -- they can just stay thoughts or they can
become our reality.

We all have learning experiences in life (some call
them mistakes). What we are is a result of how
we've learned from all of the experiences we've
encountered throughout our life. When we have
not learned sufficiently, the Universe will see fit to
give us a repeat of certain lessons until we've
become proficient from within, and then we move
on to new and different experiences.

We always have a choice . . .

It is a privilege and an honor to be living this life,
not an entitlement.

Remember the feeling you had when something really good happened in your life and you felt like you were on top of the world? Hold on to that feeling today and carry it around with you. Be consciously aware of it. If you find yourself slipping out of it, bring yourself back to that good-feeling place. See how your day goes . . .

Our lives are such beautiful tapestries of people, places and things weaving in and out of it.

We all need to find our middle ground, to find and do what makes us happy, which in turn, will empower us to live our lives in harmony.

We are all part of a divine plan. Though it's difficult (and that may be putting it mildly) to have faith that we are all being taken care of by the divine when we're in the middle of seemingly insurmountable challenges, do your best to remember that the god of your understanding (or Universe, or whatever you choose to call your belief) is watching over you and taking care of you. We are always being enfolded by divine love. It is usually our humanness (our fears, insecurities, etc.) that get in the way of moving forward in life.

The Universe has taught me that life is very fleeting and oh too short . . . so what the heck is anyone waiting for? Enjoy everything that you can while you can . . . we're only here for the blink of an eye.

Friends are an import part of life. Always be there for your friends even if it seems as if they're not always there for you. We shouldn't base our behavior on what someone else does. Being true to oneself is important.

Next time you find yourself judging another, try regrouping yourself and being more accepting.

Focus on what you DO want in anything rather than what you don't want. You will attract to you whatever your focus is. If you say that you don't want something, that's probably what you'll receive, as that's where you've given your energy. Focus on the DO's of life !!!

Fear is just another four letter word. So is Hope.

It's interesting how people ask you for your opinion on things and when you're honest with them, they get angry with you because they often don't want to face the truth -- that they have to look within for their answer(s).

I often advise people to move forward in their life. Perhaps I've misspoken. Any movement is forward movement . . . it's our mind and our thoughts that keep us stagnant. Living in our heads and holding on to the past can make movement in the present a little challenging sometimes.

Sometimes acting "as if" can be a great help in getting through a difficult day or a difficult time in your life. If you act as if you're happy, chances are your day will be brighter and you will bring yourself out of your funk. Acting "as if" can be a useful tool in changing your mood.

Living & thinking outside of the box has brought me to a wonderful place of self-love & self-acceptance. Yes, I've worked hard to be where I am now. I have accomplished more than I could ever have imagined. I continue to learn, grow, be an individual, create, and love . . . how beautiful is it to live a life free from fear, shame, guilt? It's amazingly beautiful. I am truly blessed.

We all encounter a blockage in our energy flow from time to time. Take a moment to understand where that blockage is coming from (I'll give you a hint -- it's usually from our very own attitude) and change the blockage into a challenge!!! Changing our attitude about most things will bring about a different result and most likely diffuse that blockage.

There is absolutely no such thing as an expert in anything -- we are all students and we are all teachers, all of us having different knowledge and experiences. Sure, someone may know a little more than someone else regarding a particular subject, but the other person may also know more about something completely different -- there's a balance.

LIVE your truth and be true to yourself. The tough part for some is to remember that each of us has a different truth. Some tend to be judgmental because someone else has a different belief system than they do.

We can learn a lot from mother nature. Watching how the tides flow, the seasons change, the weather gives us rain and sunshine . . . They are all indicative of how our lives ARE ... We are all energy and have ebbs and flows (yin and yang) of energy, just as the tides have high and low tide -- our bodies and emotions have the same flow of energy. There is always a balance. You know -- you need to the darkness to have light and vice versa. The important thing to remember is that we have choices to make in our lives. By living in love and gratitude, we can be on a more even keel of life and not have extreme ups and downs.

People often say I wish I could do this or that. What's stopping you? What's stopping you is that what you "wish" you could do either all the time or more often, is not yet a priority in your life. When something becomes a priority in your life, it becomes important enough for you to take action and do it !!!!

Sometimes it's challenging to keep on having faith and to know that The Universe has a grand plan for us of which we are all a part. Just sayin' that sometimes it's challenging.
Once you love yourself, the rest will fall into place.

Know expectations, know disappointments. No expectations, no disappointments.

The only thing certain in life is life's uncertainties.

People who are feeling guilty about something are usually the ones speaking about situations in which they feel they must either defend their position or bad-mouth others. It is best to send prayers of love to others and to be grateful for lessons learned.

Some people seem to enjoy making mountains out of molehills. I suppose they're used to living their lives like that. Personally, I prefer to look at the mountains and molehills and embrace them for their true values . . .

Relationships can be difficult -- all relationships -- whether it be with your teacher, hairdresser, spouse, mechanic, child -- whatever the relationship, it can be challenging at times. We must learn to be kind, loving and compassionate towards each other.

Everyone seems so quick to pass judgment. We need to open ourselves up to the possibilities of things that have been beyond our current perception.

Some people spend their time trying instead of doing. Some people spend their time searching instead of being. Either way, trying or searching -- you can't live in love and gratitude in the present. Remember to live each day in love and gratitude for what you have, and the blessings will abound!!!

I used to think that our life's journey began at birth, and I suppose it does – at least to a certain extent. Our journeys in life truly begin when we begin to face challenges, have new experiences and learn from our experiences.

I am so blessed and grateful that I have learned to let people own their own stuff -- their own

attitudes, their own drama, their own emotions --
and I don't have to be entangled in their web.

Putting into practice one's spiritual principles can
often be difficult. I am very grateful to live my life
in love and gratitude. Sure, I'm human -- I
sometimes have to pull back the reins, regroup,
and send others love when I feel like doing or
saying something else. When others choose to
live their love in anger and/or fear, their actions in
life correspond with their emotions. Sending love
and blessings to all . . . especially those who have
yet to be enlightened . . .

We should never make an assumption that
someone knows or doesn't know something based
upon our perception of their life's experience. Our
experience and opportunities in life have taught us
much and continue to teach us as we continue on
our path.

We attract what we focus on. If we focus on our
fears and anger, we will become more fearful and
angrier. If we focus on love and blessings, we will
become filled with love and gratitude.

Being a winner means that you're always learning
something from your experiences in life. I'm
always a winner!

Rather than making assumptions, ask questions
so that you can be informed rather than
presumptuous.

When the Universe has seen fit to bring you some
unexpected challenges, remember that most

challenges in life are unexpected – some are a little easier to handle than others. It's not like we specifically ask to have a broken leg or most other things in our lives that are tough to handle.

Every person, every situation, every heartache, every laugh is an experience that can teach us something in life . . . we may not know immediately what that lesson is, but eventually we will get it!

When we write something, a letter for instance, what we want to say is clear in our mind and we do our best to put it down into writing. For me, I know that there are some short circuits there and my words can sometimes get a little scrambled in the translation from my brain to my fingertips. I do my best to be as precise as possible and to express myself as accurately as I can when using the written word.

We are not even as big as a grain of sand in comparison to the Universe. Doesn't that put a perspective on things -- I mean how important anything really is in life? We need to be kinder to one another, more loving towards each other, live in the now . . .

Too many younger people today lack respect for their elders, yet they feel they're entitled to receive that very same respect. I respect those older than I am because they've lived longer than I have and because they have more experience in life than I have. In my book, younger folk must earn my respect by being respectful toward others.

I am blessed to live my life in peace, filled with love and gratitude. I wish I could bottle this up and give it away to anyone who feels the need . . . In the meanwhile, I send and give everyone love and blessings.

Some people take life a little too seriously not realizing that it's all over in the mere blink of an eye. Enjoy every moment . . . Enjoy every blessing . . . be grateful for what you have.

5 +5 = 10, 2 + 8 = 10, 6 + 4 = 10, 9 + 1 + 10. The point here is that there is always more than just one way to achieve the same goal. Just because we only know one way, doesn't mean that's the ONLY way!

Everything has a yin and a yang. You know the old adage – there are two sides to every story. There is always a light to a dark, black to white, right to wrong, good to bad, or sometimes, they are just different, not making them anything but that – different.

Have you ever noticed that some people just love living in their drama?

Everyone seems so willing to have negative "opinions" about things when in reality, they don't have all the facts. Opinions are often the product of the belief systems that we were brought up with or habits we've developed throughout our lives. Ask questions. Learn.

When others point fingers at us, we need to look inside of ourselves whether or not we perceive any wrong doing on our part.

When we are judgmental of others, there is usually something inside of us that we need to examine. When we are loving and accepting towards others, we usually have inner peace.

Be cautious about acting in haste -- once you do something it cannot be undone and can become a far more difficult situation!!

It is very freeing to live without judging others, loving unconditionally and realizing that everyone has their own path in life. Once we let go of our fears and judgments, everything becomes much "lighter." It's important to not take life too seriously . . .

Have you ever noticed how some people like to live in their anger and misery? Rather than following a path filled with love, they prefer to hold on to anger, hatred, fear – perpetuating the very thing(s) they say that they "hate." Just an interesting observation.

Life is pretty much as open as we are and living in love and gratitude allows me to spread around love, joy, and peace while not dwelling on things about which I can do nothing !!!! It's very important to let go of what we have no control over and send them on their way with a loving prayer.

The thread of life weaves such a beautiful tapestry around us, of which we are all privileged to be a part. Some of the stitches in the tapestry are longer and more complex; some are more decorative, yet they are all part of the same woven tapestry of life.

We've always had people in our life to teach you lessons when we've been ready to learn them.

Stand in one spot. Draw an imaginary circle around where you're standing - better yet, step into the center of a hula hoop that's laying on the ground. You are responsible for everything inside that hula hoop (or circle). Everything outside of that circle is not your responsibility. Now put it into practice!!!

There are always many lessons to be learned and sometimes we're hit over the head a few times in order to learn them. But, then, there are many who are not spiritually inclined who will NEVER understand their lessons during this lifetime . . . .and we all know or have known some of those who lack spirituality.

I find it astounding that some people still look outside of themselves for happiness. It saddens me that many still don't know that their joy and happiness in life lies within.

Making a judgment about someone based upon what your perception is, is not always the best route to take. If someone acts out of religious or personal beliefs, does that make it any different than acting out of orders they have received from their doctor, for instance? I think not – the only difference is in your own acceptance, which is completely conditioned upon what you think is right or wrong. It's high time we lived with unconditional love and acceptance of others.

Some people seem to thrive upon holding on to anger or negativity. It is so much easier to realize that anger or negativity is just not worth holding on to. All it takes is a shift in our attitude to live in love and gratitude.

I marvel in the ability to create my own reality within my imagination. Sure I have to live in the "real world." But that doesn't mean that while plugging along from day to day I can't get lost in my mind and create a wonderfully fun place in which to live. Being in my mind is fun. No one really knows what's going on in there except for me.

We really need to be conscious of our intent with what we say. What is the purpose of the words we want to say? Are they potentially hurtful? Do they serve a positive purpose? Be aware of your words. Be aware of what you say and how you say it. And be aware of your intent . . . what are you hoping to accomplish with what you're saying . . . .I do my best to say something positive and to make someone feel better about themselves or to make them a little happier. And, yes, I do have to think before I speak !!!

When you look for the "whys" in life, to me it implies that you're judgmental. Depending on the reason for something, it will either be acceptable to you or unacceptable to you. If you love and

accept unconditionally, the "whys" in life don't
really matter.

We can be hurt by the words and actions of
others, but we can't let those words and actions
run our lives.

There is a tendency for us to become complacent
with things in our lives. We think that people we
know will always be there. We expect that our
jobs will always be there. We expect our pets will
always be there. Until one day when they're not
there. A loved one, a pet, a job -- can all be gone
in the blink of an eye. Appreciate what you have
when you have it. Life is way too short.

Choices. It is one's choice to be happy, or not. It
is one's choice to be loving or to hold on to anger.
It is one's choice to be grateful or fearful. We have
the ability to choose what we want to be. I choose
to live in love and gratitude. I wish I could spread
love and gratitude all over like fairy dust !!!!!

Life is way too short . . . live in love, and if you're
not there yet, know that you are loved . . .

As we get older, we tend to let go of perfectionism.
We begin to realize that it's important just to do
things, whether or not they're done perfectly. That
doesn't mean we don't still strive for perfection, it
just means that our level of "perfect" is much more
relaxed with age and we realize that the challenge
lies within getting anything done rather than doing
everything perfectly.

When we're in our youth, the term "pick your battles" doesn't necessarily mean that much. I don't think we've had enough experience in life to really understand the meaning. As we mature, we begin to realize that there are very few things in life worth arguing about. We learn to agree to disagree and that we are all a little different -- that there is more than just one way to do or say anything.

I was just looking at a post about the size of the planets in our solar system and their sizes in relation to each other, the sun (our very own personal star) and other mega-stars, which are way huge. This tidbit also said that there are a hundred billion galaxies out there, which is far more than I can comprehend. At the very end, there was the "you are here" (the tiniest of dots) in relation to The Universe, and the words came up "you are not the center of The Universe." It made me think a little bit about what people deem as important on this earthly plane.

The first day of spring. What does spring represent? Let's look at what happens in spring. The awakening of the flowers -- they begin to pop up out of the ground and bloom, where they have slept during the fall and winter. The trees begin to bud -- hints of new life where there had been dormancy. The birds begin to sing, where they had been mostly silent during the cold winter months. Spring begins a new cycle of life. A cycle of new birth, new growth, new love . . . Let's try to carry that with us in our lives -- the "renewal" of spring in everything we do and feel. Let this springtime be a chance for mending that which has been broken. Let this springtime be filled with abundant renewal in everything.

Rather than making assumptions based upon mis-perceptions you may have, communicate -- speak with someone to find out what is really going on and express what you're thinking or feeling before making a mis-perceived assumption.

Social media and texting are great ways of sending brief notes, but to really communicate, you must speak with people. So much can be misunderstood and misinterpreted in the written word to each other -- one's emotional state is subject to interpretation (or misinterpretation). In writing, you can't always tell if one is writing something amidst tears or devoid of emotion. When you communicate with one another on a personal level, it is easier to understand what another person is saying and feeling, and we are less subject to misinterpret words and to allow ill-feelings to be created.

Many of us will be (or already have been) rejected by our "friends," acquaintances or even family members, because we may have a different belief system or because we may do things differently than they do. There is always more than one way -- more than one way of doing something, saying something, believing in something . . . I'm grateful that I can be true to myself and live in a place from within that is filled with unconditional love and acceptance of others, even when others may not feel the same. But then, I suppose that's the real test -- to feel that unconditional love and acceptance always, regardless of how you are perceived by others.

When we have a problem with something or someone, we must look within to see why we're reacting to a situation or to someone the way we are. When someone else has a problem with something or someone, we must realize that we have no control over changing that person or the situation. At best, we can listen to someone with love and compassion, but we can only change what is within ourselves.

Sometimes we need to just face our fears head on. Dive into your fears. Most of the time, what you have created in your head is not nearly as frightful as reality. Fantasies are a little different. Fantasies are not usually as good in reality as they are in our minds!!

Timing in life is everything. The other day, we saw a bald eagle as it was soaring down the river about a mile from where we live. Before we left home, my husband had to get out of the car to get his sunglasses. Had he not done this, we would have missed the bald eagle. It is often challenging to us to have faith that we are all being divinely guided in even the most menial of tasks (think sunglasses). All I can say is think bald eagle.

Some people go through life wondering why things happen to them. We must always keep in mind that we get what we attract. So, if you want different things to happen in your life, change how you think, change how you act, change your attitude!

Some people like to judge a book by its cover.
Other people like to understand the content.

Many people enjoy jumping to conclusions and
making assumptions. After all, you can turn pretty
much any situation around to be quite self-serving
based upon your own personal judgments.

Pretty much every parent has done the best that
they can in influencing their children in a positive
way. Some people are more limited in their
resources than others. Some people are just nicer
than others. It seems to be happening with more
regularity that people who are somewhat "off" are
becoming more prevalent in our society. I can't
help but wonder that upbringing has had little to do
with negative influences, but rather more external
sources are heavily contributing to negative
energy in our beloved children.

When we feel uncomfortable with people or a
situation, we must look within. The problem is not
usually outside of you. Both the problem and the
solution lie within.
Anger is usually a perception of what someone
has done or a way someone has acted. Most
often our perception is off and completely
inaccurate. Our perception being judgment,
whether it be of others or ourselves.

Learn to say thank you to someone rather than "I
know" or whatever other reaction you might have
to what they're saying to you. Be consciously
aware of your reactions to various situations
(wherever and whatever they may be) and catch

yourself before you react to what someone says to you, allowing a change from within yourself to take place.

It's often easier for us to create justification and validation of our feelings in our own minds, festering our anger, rather than to live in love and compassion for what someone else may be experiencing in their life.

We don't realize it but we're experts on letting go. From early childhood, we've had to let go of each school year that passed, pets that have left us, friends and/or relatives that have moved away from us -- relationships . . . Letting go is something we do throughout our lives. We have deaths -- of people, pets; we all move on from an old job or an old lifestyles; as we get older, our youth is something we have to learn to let go, Sometimes, just letting go of your favorite, "most comfortable in the whole wide world" pair of shoes is something we have to let go. Even though we're so adept at letting go, have you ever noticed that it's sometimes really difficult to do?

Many of us are resistant to change. But we have to remember the goodness about change. We're all happy when we see the first flowers of spring bloom, knowing that the weather is warming up from our cold winter nights. We feel very similar when fall brings its crisp, clean, cooler air to bring us relief from the summer's seemingly unbearable heat. The blessings from changes in our lives may not seem obvious to us at first, but they're there nonetheless.

The more I see how others behave in life, the more I am grateful for being me. Thank you Universe.

Everything we are and everything we do is a choice. We choose to be happy or not. We choose to be motivated or not. We make choices. I'm not saying it's always easy, but you CAN choose to be happy. It's up to you.

It's very easy to blame someone else for your decisions in life when there's something that you don't want to face or don't want to do.

I'm so grateful that I live my life in love, gratitude and acceptance. I continuously pray for those not yet there -- always sending them love. I'm grateful that I continuously seek to be the best me I can be, always looking to learn and grow. I'm grateful that I can let go of people and situations that are not in my best interest, yet do so with love, not with bitterness or anger. Living in love, gratitude and unconditional acceptance is the way to be happy.

If you expect things in life, you are setting yourself up for potential disappointment when those expectations are not met. If you expect nothing in life, everything you receive is an unexpected gift and a blessing.

Life's circumstances are in a constant state of flux. As we get older, hopes, dreams, desires don't go away, but there is a certain maturity that takes place as you age. Somehow, you look at the world a little differently. You realize the rich tapestry of your life and how the people and situations in your life have created that tapestry. People (and circumstances) weave in and out of your life making the rich embroidered picture of your reality that unfolds as your life, and manifests in what you become as a person. Every circumstance in your life, every person with whom you have crossed paths, every event that you have been a part of, everything that has happened to you, everything in your life no matter how big or small, all have made you, you. Be grateful for all of it – even what you consider "bad" – because even the "bad" in your life has given you the opportunity to grow and become a better you.

We're all on a different page in our life's story. That's what makes the book of life so interesting.

Remember: The only thing in our lives that is permanent is change. Embrace that change as part of our human evolution, knowing that it's part of our life's journey and all a part of helping us to become the best that we can be.

Does anyone else have things in their lives that have happened to them that you just can't forget? Sure, you've moved passed them, worked through them, but because of what's happened, you're always guarded or very cautious around certain people that could still be in your life or situations that you will not forget. Forgiving and forgetting are quite different.

I won't stop being your friend because we have different belief systems, whether it be religious, political or anything else. I will not attack you verbally by calling you names because of our differences. I will not gossip about you because we are different. Our differences in life are what make us unique. We all live on this planet together and hopefully we can find a common sandbox to play in together.

Often when we see that someone "needs" to act a certain way, or do something other than what they're doing, it's a sign that we need to be doing that very same thing that we're observing and thinking that the other person needs to be doing. We can usually live our lives by setting an example rather than by telling someone what THEY should be doing.

As long as I can look at everything that happens in my life as an experience from which I can learn, I'm doing OK. Though I live my life in love and gratitude, there are times when I'm human and I let my emotions get the better of me. It doesn't make me less grateful or less filled with love, it makes me human.

Be mindful of what you say and how you say it. There is no reason to be unkind to one another, even if we may disagree on things. Love, kindness, gratitude all win in the end. Let's be more loving towards each other.

Someone once said that all publicity is good publicity, just as long as people are talking about you. That means they're noticing you. From that, we give whatever it is that we're talking about or

whomever it is we're talking about . . . energy.
When we give something energy, we perpetuate it.

We've all taken baby steps to get to where we are
today. Some of us need more baby steps, some of
us need less baby steps. The fact remains that
we're all fulfilling our destinies in the best way we
know how to do so.

When we feel uncomfortable around someone or
don't like someone, it's usually a reflection of
something within that we're seeing. Our discomfort
usually has no bearing on the other person and
isn't related to them at all. We have to learn to own
our own emotions and to look within for healing.

I choose to live in an endless realm of possibilities,
keeping open to the blessings that The Universe has
the ever flowing potential to bestow upon us, by
continuously repeating What Else Is Possible...

Holding on to anger and/or hurt takes so much effort. If
you turn that anger/hurt to love and blessings, and
gratitude for the lessons you've learned -- whatever they
may be -- it's as if a weight has been lifted off your
shoulders.

We all grow and evolve in our own time. The pulse of that
evolution within creates the vibrations around us and
keep the world running. We should never compare
ourselves with anyone else's evolutionary path, as we all
grow at our own rate. It's kind of like planting a seed. We
can plant two identical flower seeds in the ground and
they may germinate at different times, bloom at different
times -- some with more flowers and the other with less
flowers -- but they're still evolving and growing at their
own rate, both participating in the heartbeat of The
Universe.

What causes us to become angry or upset with someone? Is it really because of something we perceive that they did or is it something within ourselves that we need to examine? I always look within and do my best to change me on the inside, because when I am upset or angered with a situation or a person, that anger belongs only to me. It tells me that something within needs a little work.

Isn't it better to speak with someone directly about something that may be bothering you because of something you perceived rather than to let that misguided thought or perception fester, as if it is an infection in our minds?

Imagination can be an amazing tool. Picturing rainbow colored unicorns running in a field of flowers with glittering sunshine sparkling down upon them can instantly lift one's spirit. But, when we spend too much time in our heads fostering negative scenarios and situations that we are creating in our minds and are not reality based, our mood can quickly take a down turn. That is when we usually try to blame something or someone outside of ourselves for what we're feeling rather than taking responsibility for creating our own reality from within, which is usually fear based. Letting go of situations over which we have no control, accepting what is; releasing anger, fear, stress, negativity, are all helpful in adjusting our attitude towards anything. And what is the only thing over which we have control? You all know the answer to this – our own attitude !!! Everything outside of that doesn't belong to us. Keep that in mind the next time you're "bothered" by something – where does that fall in your life? Is it within your own hula hoop or something outside of your hula hoop? I've said it before and I'll say it again, living life in unconditional acceptance, love and gratitude as much as you can is the best way to keep moving forward in your life.

We must open our eyes to the rainbows of the universe
and watch the colors dance before us.

I love you,

Jane